M000073080

The Still Small Voice

Robert Weston

A Pilgrim's Guide to

Listening to the Lord

New Wine Press

New Wine Ministries
PO Box 17
Chichester
West Sussex
United Kingdom
PO19 2AW

Copyright © 2006 Robert Weston

All rights reserved. No part of this publication may be reproduced, stored in a retrieval system, or transmitted in any form or by any means, electronic, mechanical, photocopying or otherwise, without the prior written consent of the publisher. Short extracts may be used for review purposes.

Scripture quotations are taken from the following versions of the Bible:

NIV - The HOLY BIBLE, NEW INTERNATIONAL VERSION
Copyright © 1973, 1978, 1984 by International Bible Society.
Used by permission of Hodder and Stoughton Limited.

HOLY BIBLE, NEW LIVING TRANSLATION.
Copyright © 1996. Used by permission of Tyndale House Publishers, Inc. Wheaton, Illinois 60189. All rights reserved.

ISBN 1-903725-62-3

Typeset by Ruach Breath of Life Ministries
www.ruachministries.org
Cover photograph taken in Jersey by Robert Weston
Design by Hannah Prittie & John Weston
Shetland, Devon and Shropshire

Printed in Malta

Phil Buechler writes . . .

'There are few subjects that attract people's attention so much as how we can hear God's voice. As an international Bible teacher, who has taught on this subject many times, I highly recommend this book for its excellent teaching, as well as my knowledge of Robert's heart, experience and high standards.

I was sent the pre-publication manuscript for review during a hectic holiday season. At best I hoped to be able to skim through it, then do a quick write up in order to express what I know about the author – he is the "real deal" – and what I could glean from a quick read through. It didn't work out as planned. I devoured the manuscript. I savored sentence after sentence. I stopped to pray when inspired, to repent when convicted, to rejoice when illumination for a longstanding question had been given, and to seek the Lord when a new question emerged.

This book will aid you in drawing closer to Him, and help you to walk out His leadings with a sense of wonder and childlike adventure.' (Phil Buechler, *Phil Buechler Ministries,* Memphis.)

Other commendations for The Still Small Voice

'Powerful! I believe this anointed book is crucial for the Body of Christ. Robert's ability to entwine his personal experience with practical life application erases the mystery from communicating with God, and simplifies a subject that is often overcomplicated. This book encourages us to delve into a deeper adventure with the Lord, and will free multitudes from feeling intimidated about hearing God's voice. After reading *The Still Small Voice*, I feel like I've been born again – again!' (Therese Marszalek, *Miracles still happen* and *Miracles of the Master,* Harrison House.)

'It fans the flames of longing for closeness with His heart, and through it, His Presence pulls me to my knees.' (Sally Mowbray, *Ruach Breath of Life Ministries*)

TO

ROSALIND

MY WIFE, AND PARTNER IN LISTENING

FOR TWENTY-THREE YEARS

ACKNOWLEDGEMENTS

Our gratitude goes to the many who have read at least some part of this manuscript at some stage of its long gestation, including:

Sally Mowbray and Stephen James Pigott, (SJ), who were closely involved in the successive drafts of this book; my father, John Weston, for much help with the formatting; Francis and Lindsey Cummings, precious friends up north, Liz Allen, a wonderful friend close by; Roger and Angie Allen of Christian Aid; Janet Keeling, Jacqui Hyde, Kate Theobald, Rhea Morgan, Hilary Ashton and her sister Jennie Rimmer who pastors the church William Carey once preached in; Debbie le Sueur and Mike Field, who directs the prayer initiatives on Jersey, which is where I took the front cover photograph.

In the United States, our love to Phil Buechler, Therese Marszalek, Rosalie Willis and those trusty stalwarts, Paul and Gretel Haglin. Special thanks to Hannah Prittie for her work in designing the back cover, and to Tréva Solanki and Laurie Klein for their superb proof-reading. Any mistakes that have got through are the results of my own last minute tampering with the text.

At the publishers' request, we have Americanized the spelling and punctuation. We would ask British readers to be forbearing!

Contents

Foreword

'The Still Small Voice is written with simplicity and elegance by a pilgrim for pilgrims. It combines practical counsel with devotion, marrying a depth of Scriptural insight with the wisdom of the Holy Spirit. I found it inspiring and encouraging, bringing fresh and renewed light into my soul.

This Pilgrim's Guide to Listening to the Lord is full of balance and sound good sense. It is the fruit of someone who has sought long and hard to understand the Lord's ways of communicating.

It explores many of the diverse ways God speaks: in dreams, visions, nudges and through silence. Robert helps us understand times of drought and delay and addresses, amongst many other issues, the perennial problems of disappointment, disillusionment, deception, warfare and confusion concerning timing. It is particularly excellent on discernment and waiting on God.

At the same time it moves the reader away from 'listening' as a purely personal pusuit, and places it in the context of hearing God's heart and strategy for His world.

The times *For Reflection and Prayer* at the end of each segment help to establish a rhythm of response to the teaching, and also to distil one's own thoughts, making sure that the information gets quickly turned into prayer.

I found the guide *really* helpful, with Robert and Rosalind emerging from its pages as seasoned and trustworthy guides for the journey.

You will find fresh confidence to believe that you can hear God, and wise instruction on how to be more sensitive to the Still Small Voice of God. I commend it to you.'

Revd Paul Miller
World Prayer Center and New Day Ministries

Introduction

Imagine the Bible shorn of all references to the Lord speaking directly. We would be left with no key to understand *why* the historical episodes relating to Moses, Joshua, David and the like happened. We would be none the wiser as to *who* had initiated them or *what* they were pointing to. Our spiritual understanding would be severely impoverished.

One word from heaven is worth a dozen of our own bright ideas. The whole history of the Bible is of the Lord taking hold of people's lives and directing them to attempt things they could never have achieved by their own efforts. He loves to speak to His children!

'The Still Small Voice' of God births visions, counteracts unbelief, overcomes prejudices, dispels confusion, restores joy and enables us to find fresh direction – even if we have taken wrong turnings in the past.

Martin Luther declared that God only speaks 'baby talk' to us, because that is all we are capable of understanding. With considerable trepidation, I have set out to show that the Lord can take us beyond 'baby speak' to the point where He can share more of His heart with us.

Does this mean we need to be high flying prophets to hear anything of value? By no means. Even those we look up to in Scripture as giants of faith have their flaws – sometimes gaping ones. Deuteronomy 30:14 reassures us, however, that *The word is very near you; it is in your mouth and in your heart, so you may obey it.*

The best way to use this book is to take as much time as you can to turn the teaching, as well as the meditations, into prayer. As you do so, may the Still Small Voice refresh your spirits, enlarge your vision and make your days more and more a heavenly adventure. The urgency of our times, and the Lord's own longing, require no less.

Robert Weston, Shetland and Devon

As we start

Oh let me hear Thee speaking, in accents clear and still,
Above the storms of passion, the murmurs of self will;
O speak to reassure me, to hasten or control;
O speak, and make me listen, thou guardian of my soul.

John Ernest Bode

As we start on this journey, Lord,
may Your presence be close at hand.

We long to meet with You today, Lord;
in the stillness draw near.

We throw open the doors of our heart,
and celebrate the love that calls us to Your service.

May the grace of Christ light our paths;
our journeys and encounters,
our hopes and our dreams.

We offer them, Lord, to You:
direct them where You will for Your glory.

As we embark in the flow of your Spirit's leading,
unlock the springs of creativity in our hearts –
ideas and inspiration that flow to Your glory.

Let the power of God rise up as we worship,
the love of God as we reach out to others,
and the joy of Christ as we live this day for You.

Chapter One

Come and Listen

> Jesus took with him Peter, James and John the brother of
> James, and led them up a high mountain by themselves.
> There he was transfigured before them. His face shone like
> the sun, and his clothes became as white as the light. Just
> then there appeared before them Moses and Elijah, talking
> with Jesus.   (Matthew 17:1-2)

What a breakthrough! Peter had finally recognized that Jesus
really was the Christ of God – and it led to Jesus taking him
up a high mountain to pray, along with two other favored
disciples, James and John.

The three of them must have wondered what the trip was
all about. If Jesus was going to teach and feed the multitudes
again, then where were all the crowds? Why bother traipsing
up a mountainside when there were so many needy people in
the towns and villages clamoring for attention?

They had no idea they were about to witness something
still more wonderful than when Heaven had opened at Jesus'
baptism.[1] The Father was about to reconfirm the seal of
approval He had previously placed on his Son. The appearance of His face changed, His face shone like the sun, and His
clothes became as white as the light, as bright as a flash of
lightning. Moses and Elijah conversed with Jesus – and in a
moment the Father would speak from heaven.

The call to come higher

> Peter said to Jesus, "Lord, it is good for us to be here. If you
> wish, I will put up three shelters – one for you, one for
> Moses and one for Elijah." While he was still speaking, a
> bright cloud enveloped them, and a voice from the cloud

said, "This is my Son, whom I love; with him I am well pleased. Listen to him!" When the disciples heard this, they fell face down to the ground, terrified. But Jesus came and touched them. "Get up," he said. "Don't be afraid." (Matthew 17:3-7)

The Cross was already beginning to cast its long shadow when Jesus led Peter, James and John up the high mountain. Knowing the difficult path that lay ahead, Jesus Himself would have been strengthened by this experience – but the word from Heaven was primarily for the benefit of the disciples.

Notice particularly what the Father did not say, 'Pray to Him,' because Jesus had already taught them how to pray. He said, 'Listen to Him.' He would not have said this had it not been *possible* for them to do so.

For Reflection and Prayer
Lord, on the slopes of Mount Hermon
You showed the disciples how much You love Your Son.
We heed the words the Father spoke from Heaven,
and let the realization of who You really are
penetrate still deeper in our heart.
At any moment , Lord,
Your power and presence
can break through.
So suddenly Your glory came:
one moment a bare mountain,
and then the veil parted as
Heaven came to earth.
Shekinah glory flooded the mountainside,
fills both Heaven and Earth.
You are surrounded with glory, Lord Jesus –
and so by Your mercy are we.

The Lord confides in those who fear Him

The Lord confides in those who fear Him.
He takes the upright into His confidence.
                    (Psalm 25:14, Proverbs 3:32)

In the midst of a world where so many who use the name of God as little more than a swear word, can you sense how precious it is to the Lord when He finds someone – better still a whole fellowship – willing to share the things that are on His heart?

As we turn away from life's many distractions and 'follow Jesus up the mountainside' – even by taking a few minutes out of a busy schedule – we become more aware of Heaven's perspective, and are better equipped to face life's challenges.

Just as we may share our greatest joys with many, but only reveal our greatest trials and difficulties with those we trust and feel most comfortable with, so Jesus took 'the inner three' (Peter, James and John) up the mountain in order that they should see Him as He really was: the Lord of Glory. This was doubly important, because the forthcoming ordeal might appear to make Jesus look like nothing more than a battered victim.

Just as parents long for the day when they can take their children more fully into their confidence, so the Lord wants to share how He feels with us – whether about personal, political, spiritual or environmental issues.

'You are those who have stood by me in my trials', Jesus assured His disciples, at what we now call the Last Supper. 'I have eagerly desired to eat this meal with you.'[2] He grieves when such closeness with His people is missing.

In every century there have been those who have loved Jesus with all their hearts. One such was Margery Kempe. The Lord spoke often to this woman, who gave her all to Him. Back in the fourteenth century she wrote, 'In my soul I heard Jesus say, "I ask no more of you than that you love Me as I love you. I would take you by the hand so that people know that you are My friend. I would speak to you more often than you will let Me."' Would He not say same something similar to us?

For Reflection and Prayer

At the height of the persecution in the Soviet Union, a man imprisoned for his faith penned a highly challenging note.

Smuggled out of a concentration camp it reached believers in the West. 'Yes,' it read, 'our main need *is* for prayer – but lead such lives that God can answer your prayers.'

> *We agree together, Lord:*
> *do whatever it takes*
> *to make us into people who lead such lives*
> *that You can answer our prayers.*

One word from Heaven

In any situation we find ourselves in, it is good to ponder 'What would Jesus do?' It is even more prophetic to ask, 'What are You *already* doing, Lord?'

If I had to select one verse to summarize the Lord Jesus' ministry, it would be John 5:19: 'I only do what I see my Father doing.' Because Jesus listened constantly to the Still Small Voice, He knew what to do in any given situation. As a result, the blind saw and the deaf heard.

The briefest word from Heaven can bring about the most far-reaching effects. When the Lord spoke on the road to Damascus, Saul the Persecutor became overnight a devoted follower of Christ. The Holy Spirit spoke again at Antioch[3], summoning Paul to his apostolic calling. Because the Lord spoke, and the disciples heeded the Still Small Voice, churches were planted wherever they went.

Only Eternity will reveal the full story of *whom* the Lord has spoken to, and *how* He has worked His purposes out. The most ordinary people have received the most surprising and challenging assignments.

Only the Lord knows, too, all the fruit that will come as a result of the words that He has spoken to you.

For Reflection and Prayer

Have you ever felt a bit disappointed by the disciples' reaction to the Transfiguration? Befuddled by sleep and decidedly fearful, they were desperate to preserve this remarkable moment. Peter's suggestion of building high altitude booths seems somewhat wooden, but when you consider what a decisive leader he became later on – and how slow we often are to respond to the Spirit's leading – our impatience disappears. We are meant to be at home in God's presence, but what He does will often take us by surprise.

The most important thing is to open ourselves to God's leading, and not to let fear in. He is not going to send us to darkest Peru. I made this point in a meeting once, and a lady put her hand up. 'He did!' she replied. Perhaps I should have said, 'He won't send us there unless it really is the best thing for both Him and us!

> *Lover of our souls, we come close now to listen.*
> *We set ourselves to follow You*
> *up the mountainside.*
> *It thrills Your heart*
> *when we give You the love of ours.*

> *Forgive us when we hold back, Lord.*
> *Lead us further on and further in.*
> *When we are caught up in Your presence,*
> *how beautiful it is.*
> *There is nowhere we would rather be.*

Word and Spirit in balance

Many years ago, Smith Wigglesworth declared that revival will come when God's people put sufficient emphasis on both Word and Spirit.

Precisely because the concept of listening to the Lord appears so experience oriented, we cannot stress too strongly from the outset that Word and Spirit *must* flow together. We are, in fact, only safe to embark on the highway of listening to the Still Small Voice if we are rooted in the Word.

Far more than through any other means of communication, it is by reading, studying and meditating on the Word of God that we hear the Still Small Voice. The only reason I am not devoting more space in this publication to this crucial topic is because other authors have covered the theme of biblical meditation so eloquently.

When Scripture 'lives' within our heart, it provides a bedrock of faith with which to meet life's many challenges. Just as many great musicians and actors claim they can only bring a piece of music or drama fully to life when they have committed it to memory, in much the same way the Word of God assumes new power and depth once it is stored in our heart.

Bishop Hans Lilje relates that it was the constant rehearsing of the psalms and hymns he had learnt as a boy that saved his hope and sanity when the Nazis placed him in solitary confinement. Watchman Nee claimed the same after spending twenty-five years in prison undergoing extreme Communist indoctrination.

Most of us, if we are honest, could do a great deal more when it comes to developing these important aspects of Scriptural meditation and memorization. There are many underused 'channels' in our brain that we could so usefully fill with the Word of God!

For Reflection and Prayer

We praise You that Your Word is living and active;
Help us to hear You through it,
now wild and disturbing, now calm and reassuring.
Let it enter the secret places of our heart,
dispersing fear and bringing light and love.
Take it deeper into the pores of our heart,
to shape our thinking and check our impulses.

Do not limit God!

'If we are careful not to limit Him, He shows up as the God who answers by fire. He sends His presence, His healing and His deliverance power.' (Suzanne Pillans)

Suzanne Pillans is a horse riding instructor who lives in Oxfordshire. Whenever circumstances permit, she responds to the Lord's call to preach the gospel and journies forth to the ends of the earth.[4]

Her first overseas work was in Malawi. Despite being poorly when she was preaching, she saw many people accept Jesus into their hearts, and receive His healing in their bodies. From there she went to preach the gospel on the Mozambique border. She was somewhat disappointed when fewer than twenty-five people showed up at the meeting.

'Don't limit God!' she reminded herself, for that was the phrase the Lord had been burning on her heart for the past few weeks. She was somewhat prepared, therefore, when the Lord said to her, 'Invite them to bring the sickest person in the village to the evening meeting. Let them come and watch Jesus heal them.'

That night the church was packed as the villagers brought someone along who had not been out of bed for two years and who could neither stand nor walk. 'Sickness, leave in Jesus' Name,' Suzanne commanded. 'Body, be healed in Jesus' Name. Strength, come back in Jesus' Name. In the Name of Jesus stand up!'

The lady stood to her feet and walked. 'Now,' Suzanne commanded, 'in the Name of Jesus, run down the aisle and back again!' The lady looked at Suzanne in horror. 'In Jesus' Name you can do it,' she reassured her. The lady took off and ran down the aisle and back again.

As a result of seeing this miraculous healing, all the people present became Christians, and continued worshipping the Lord until three o'clock in the morning.

The following day two deaf and mute girls received Jesus into their lives and were also miraculously healed. They are now learning to speak.

None of these events would have come about had Suzanne settled for the self-evident 'fact' that African villagers do not turn out en masse to listen to little known visiting female evangelists. It was because she listened to the Still Small Voice that the Lord Jesus was so immensely glorified.

Imagine how grateful you would be if you had been that sick person, and someone had come along with the spiritual authority to make you better. That is how important this theme of listening to the Lord really is.

Beyond the miracles themselves, God has a message for the Church. The Lord showed Suzanne that we in the West are *limiting* Him by our unbelief, our lack of prayer and by putting other things before Christ.

In a vision, she saw Judas Iscariot receiving the thirty pieces of silver. At that moment, he loved the silver more than Jesus. Too many of us today love our money more than Jesus, and our homes, holidays, jobs, promotions, sport and life-styles. Some of us even love our ministries more than Jesus. All of this hinders the Lord from moving in revival power.

The Lord told Suzanne to call God's people to repentance. Everywhere she goes, she preaches this message. Entire congregations have come to repentance, often with tears.

The depth of our repentance will vitally determine how far the Lord can take us as individuals and as fellowships. As we yield our lives and agendas to Him, the word of the Lord comes and He is free to move in power. With less of us and more of Him, it is so much easier for Him!

For Reflection and Prayer
Show us ways in which we are limiting You, Lord.
Lead us into a deeper repentance,
so that we may hear what You are saying.

Determination that defeats distractions

Did you ever see two romantically-challenged people who were reluctant to spend time together? If Jesus took time away from the crowds to climb a mountain and go 'on retreat,' then we must be willing to take similar measures.

It is not only on mountaintops or in special meetings that we hear the Still Small Voice. It often happens when we are at our most relaxed. 'Fallow' times are so conducive for promoting intimacy with the Lord, and for receiving His ideas, that there is everything to be said for deliberately setting aside times when we switch off our over analytical brain and *let* the Holy Spirit commune with us.

Simple steps can make our listening environment more conducive. For example, dedicating a corner of the house as a place where we seek the Lord regularly will make us want to stay there longer in His presence.

Nevertheless, listening to the Lord requires discipline and dedication as well as inspirational settings. If we need to stay up late, or rise early in order to obtain the space and seclusion we crave, then we are following in the Master's footsteps.

It is precious to spend time with the Lord at an hour when there are fewer distractions around. The more we use odd moments during the day to seek His face, the more easily we will recognize the Still Small Voice calling us to pray when we wake unexpectedly, or when He points our attention in a certain direction.

For Reflection and Prayer

Lord Jesus,
You share the heart beat of Heaven
with those who hunger and thirst for Your presence.
Come, Light that knows no night,
Infuse and quicken our dull and listless minds.
Let love push back the frontiers of our shame,
and trust grow strong where guilt once reigned.
Bid turmoil cease and hope shine through
the clutter of vain and empty thoughts –
for this makes room for You to work
and draws us close to Your heart.

References

[1] Matthew 3:16-17

[2] Luke 22:15, 28f

[3] Acts chapter 9; 13:2

[4] Material in this section has been used with Suzanne's permission. See *Dare to Step out in Faith* (New Wine, 2006) and *Miracles of the Master* (Harrison House, 2006).

The Proslogion of St Anselm

Turn away from your daily work.
Hide yourself for a little time
from your restless thought;
give yourself a little leisure to talk with God,
and rest awhile with Him.

Enter the secret chamber of your heart,
shutting out everything but God,
and that which may help you in seeking Him.
And when you've closed the door, seek Him.
Now, my whole heart, say to God:
'I seek Your face; Your face, O Lord, do I seek.'

I will seek You by desiring You,
and desire You in seeking You.
I will find You by loving You,
and love You in finding You . . .

I do not seek to understand so that I may believe,
but believe that I may understand.
For this I know to be true,
that unless I first believe
I shall not understand.

Chapter Two

Recognize His Voice

We limit ourselves when we say, 'I'm not the sort of person the Lord would speak to.' It honors Him when we attempt to listen to His Still Small Voice.

In C. S. Lewis' *Chronicles of Narnia,* the news that Aslan was on the move never failed to cheer spirits and to be greeted with wild enthusiasm. In our day, when the Lord is on the move by His Spirit, and many are hearing Him leading, warning and directing them with extreme clarity, it is vital that we *recognize* the ways by which He speaks.

May I take a certain familiarity with the basic ways in which the Lord communicates with us for granted? We have all known times when a passage from the Bible, or a Christian book, has taken on a special meaning, or when a preacher's words has spoken directly to our situation.

Such experiences reassure us of God's care. He knows what we are going through, and wants to share it with us.

We will likewise have known the Spirit's prompting to ring or visit someone at 'just the right time.' These are such familiar experiences, that it is often only with hindsight that we realize it really *was* the Lord speaking.

In this chapter, we are going to explore less the 'nuts and bolts' of how we hear God speaking so much as consider how we can gain *confidence* in recognizing the Still Small Voice. Despite the confusion we all go through in seeking God's will, the Lord wants us to be alert to His leading – and to teach young Christians to listen likewise. This is what our friend Sally Mowbray wrote about her early struggles in this respect:

When I was a younger Christian, I was constantly afraid that I was not hearing God's voice at all. Then I came across this verse in John 10:27: 'My sheep listen to My voice; I know them, and they follow Me.'

Suddenly it hit me: this was a *statement of fact.* God said it, so it must be true! It was my feelings that were off-beam. The thoughts in my head that said I could not hear God's voice were none other than the 'Father of Lies' making a determined push to have me give up even trying to listen.

When I started approaching life with the confidence and expectation that I really could hear God's voice, I found it much easier to recognize when He was speaking to me.

To help us discern the Shepherd's accents amid the mass of voices that clamor in our minds, it helps to bear in mind that the Lord speaks to our *spirit,* and with greater clarity than the *mind* produces. This may sound like a minor nuance, but it is a serious distinction. When the Spirit speaks, we are left with a deep assurance, even if we do not fully understand all the implications of what He has said. When we 'hear' only our own fears, we are usually left with nothing more substantial than a sense of confusion – or with a false euphoria if we are heeding delusory desires.

When the Lord says the very thing we most wanted to hear, it can be almost as hard to believe it as it is when He calls us to face something more challenging. We are afraid we are imagining the words of blessing and promise, just as we are inclined to rebel against warnings or rebuke.

For Reflection and Prayer

Confidence and right expectations are important aspects of listening to the Still Small Voice. Paul always had confidence that God would turn things out for the best[1] – unlike a certain king of Israel who was afraid to listen because he expected

God's prophets to say nothing good about him.[2] Which of these 'extremes'do you veer towards?

If we only expect God to rebuke us, we have a seriously distorted view of Him. Since Jesus is for us, and all He says and does is designed to bless and develop us, why side with the enemy's hopelessly jaundiced and biased assessment of situations?

Lord, I dare to believe
that Your goodness is coming towards me.[3]
What You have promised You will bring to pass. Amen!

Our ability to hear varies from day to day

Be careful to drop vain and useless thoughts the moment you become conscious of them, but quietly, without effort or violence. Abandon to Divine Providence all that might become a subject of preoccupation for you.
(Jean-Pierre de Caussade)

Did you see the film *The Heroes of Telemark?* Against all the odds, courageous Allied saboteurs destroyed stocks of heavy water that were vital to German scientists in their bid to develop an atomic bomb. Their efforts were further advanced than most people realize. Had the Nazis achieved their goal, the war would have had a very different ending. As is often the case, the real story is far more compelling than the supposedly more dramatic Hollywood version.[4]

Amongst the unsung heroes of the Resistance movement were the radio operators. These people took their lives in their hands every time they made their transmissions, running the gauntlet of sophisticated Nazi detection finding apparatus.

When radio reception was crystal clear, messages could easily be transmitted and received. On other occasions, when the static was strong, it was all but impossible to make anything out. Most of us have similar experiences when it comes to trying to listen.

It is worth recognizing from the outset that we will experience times – even prolonged ones – when we will be unable to hear anything at all. Illness deadens, the devil opposes, our flesh mishears . . . these are such common experiences that I will be devoting a whole book in the Pilgrim's Guide series to the theme of spiritual wildernesses.

On one occasion, when I was feeling particularly troubled about this, the Lord reminded me that there are seasons in the life of the soul, just as there are in nature. Even the Lord Jesus knew times when the Spirit's power was particularly strong.[5] By reverse logic, there must have been times when the power of the Lord was less present to heal.

I find it awesome how calmly the Lord Jesus coped with interruptions. Time and again, He would be on His way to accomplish one mission, when something would crop up to delay Him. May the Lord grant us discernment to tell the difference between 'God-incidences' and needless – or even demonic – interruptions.

We should take extra care with revelations that come during feverish or highly emotional interludes. Too many demands can likewise clog and confuse the wavelengths of our mind. Neither should we underestimate the furious efforts the demonic forces make to 'jam' our communication. Far better than we, they recognize the damage that will be done to their kingdom when a person, group or fellowship is following the leading of the Lord.

Although our ability to hear varies, there is often what I term a 'Five Minute Barrier' to persevere through as we try to bring our soul to stillness. During this period (which can last a great deal longer than five minutes) we may have to wrestle with all manner of wayward and disturbing thoughts. It pays to jot down the more useful of these as they come, so that we do not spend the rest of our time worrying that we will forget to license the car or to take the chicken out of the freezer.

Track down and isolate any other niggles in your soul. Decide then whether to pray specifically about them – which *might* be wisdom, but there again might only serve to play into the Distracter's hand. There are times when it is better to push such thoughts resolutely to one side. Refuse them house room!

Will we always break through the turbulence of our mental clutter and come into the unhindered presence of God? I would dearly love to say that we will, but realistically this will not always be the case.

If, after a period of time, our thoughts are refusing to settle, our spirits remain leaden, and daydreams are making serious reflection impossible, we may be wiser to leave it for the time being. Go and do something else instead.

On other occasions, we do reach a place of inner stillness only to have to drag ourselves immediately away as other duties beckon. It is better to have glimpsed and tasted than to have made no real effort to seek the Lord. Something of that inner peace will remain with us as we head into the busyness of the day.

For Reflection and Prayer

How serious are we about wanting to go deeper with the Lord? We do not *need* to allow our attention to be always taken up with worries, people and tasks-to-do. I see a picture of the Lord, alone, standing with me.

I am facing Him, but these other things are 'hangers-on', clawing at me and demanding my attention. I watch my head swivel from one to another as they catch my attention.

The interesting thing is that they are not between me and My Father; they are positioned behind and beside me so I have to turn my head away from Him in order to focus on them. I am left with my body facing the Lord, but my head turned away.

I have chosen to turn towards these distractions and give them my attention. The Lord longs for me to give Him my undivided attention – not least because He knows how much this will benefit me. (Sally Mowbray)

When the Lord dons a disguise

> As they talked and discussed these things with each other,
> Jesus Himself came up and walked along with them – but
> they were kept from recognizing Him. (Luke 24:14)

Cleopas and Mary were walking disconsolately back to
Emmaus having witnessed the crucifixion of Jesus. Suddenly,
a stranger came and kept them company. After they had
poured out their hurting hearts, He opened up the Scriptures
to them – and their hearts burned within them. There is a
simple reason why they were so slow to recognize their Lord:
Scripture says that He came to them – as He often does to us
– in a different form.[6]

When the Lord dons unexpected disguises, He always has
good reasons for doing so. In *The Horse and his Boy,* the
runaways Shasta and Aravis are riding separately by night.
Suddenly, they hear what sounds like two lions roaring on
either side of them. The lions propel the pair together and the
adventures begin. They discover later that there had only ever
been one lion – Aslan himself.[7]

Further on in the story, Aslan takes the form of a cat, in
order to comfort a boy who is obliged to spend a night
amongst haunted ruins. The boy would have been afraid of a
lion, so Aslan adopts a humbler disguise.

It sounds less than impressive to admit it, but it is not
always at all obvious whether something is of God, the devil
or just a mundane muddle. Struggling to confirm an on-line
airline ticket a few months ago, as yet another attempt came
to nothing, I felt like shouting in block capital hieroglyphics:
'What's the point of a web site you can't book tickets on?!?'

It was at this rather jaundiced moment that I sensed the Still
Small Voice prompting me to book my ticket one day *earlier*
than I had been intending. Glancing up, I saw a shining
rainbow outside my window. Minutes later the phone rang
with an invitation to attend an important meeting in the House
of Lords on that earlier day.

There I had been, blaming British Airways and the devil for the delay, whilst all the time God had been *preventing* me from wasting money on a non-refundable ticket, because He *wanted* me to be present at that meeting. When I came to book this revised date, the system worked perfectly.

In times of waiting, we are easily inclined to feel that the Lord is not doing very much. Like the disciples, we long to rouse Jesus from His sleep on the cushions of the boat![8] When we cannot make sense of a predicament, try looking away from it for a moment, and thanking Him. The Lord hears our prayers, and wants us to trust Him – even if He appears to be fast asleep, or nowhere to be seen. The more we trust, the easier it is for Him to work His purposes out.

Because there is often a significant time delay between the Lord's call and its subsequent outworking, however, there is always a danger that we will try to fulfill the vision by our own efforts. The troubles multiply when we take matters into our own hands. Like Abraham we can make an 'Ishmael' even out of genuine promises. At all such times, the guiding principle to remember is: 'Do not try to row when the wind is not filling your sails.'

If you have already jumped the gun in some area, it is never too late to repent. He hears our cries, reweaves the strands of our life and helps us to fare better next time round. By the Lord's grace, He usually does allow us further chances. He also knows us well enough to start in plenty of time!

For Reflection and Prayer

Lord Jesus, if You had come before the midnight hour,
all the virgins would have been ready.
It was the long delay which exposed their folly.
In all our times of waiting,
may our faith not fail.
When sharp frustrations come our way,
may impatience not cause us
to move ahead of Your purposes –
and may fear not cause us to hold back .

Diets that develop or diminish our hearing

> What we fill our hearts and minds with is highly likely to affect our hearing. The company we keep and the books we read will, to a large extent, determine the sort of people we will become.

The TV soaps and sitcoms do nothing to promote an eternal perspective, or to help us hear the Still Small Voice. What they can do is to make us dangerously passive, living our emotional lives through the highs and lows of these imaginary characters.

I was brought up on the BBC radio classic, *Listen with Mother*. Given the central role that television plays in most people's weekly routine, can we 'Watch with our Heavenly Father' and turn away from programs – and even conversations – that jar and jangle our spirits?

You can? That is a sure sign that your spirit is still functioning. You find it hard to reach for the off-knob? Here is a simple but possible remedy. See if the Lord is 'anointing' you for something else!

God comes to those who wait for Him, and who soak themselves in His Word. Reading, like traveling, expands our experience and increases our understanding of the ways God works.

We can learn truths from books that can inspire us to new heights, and save us from years of stumbling along wrong paths.

It is good to stock our mind by reading widely – but we can feed our spirit richer fare by slowing right down, and focusing on just a few verses of Scripture, or on some book that is speaking to our hearts.

> *Lord, please lead us to the material*
> *that we can read and watch with the heart;*
> *things that will not just inform our minds*
> *but touch and inspire our spirits,*
> *and release Your creative flow in our lives.*

For Reflection and Prayer

Turning what we have read and watched into prayer is an excellent way to share more of our lives with the Lord, and to cultivate the Still Small Voice. Reflect on some of the books that you have read in the past year or two. (Magazine or newspaper articles will do equally as well). Pray for the people who wrote them, and meditate on the subjects that they cover. Is there anyone else the Lord would have you introduce this valuable material to?

Next, recall a few special documentaries that have meant a lot to you. 'Harness' the information that has touched you,and use it as a starting point for prayer.

Listening that affirms each other

> When the rams are looking at the shepherd, their woolly coats rub companionably against each other – but when they look at each other they see only horns. (Anon)

Recognizing the work of the Spirit in each other is a vital part of being in touch with the Still Small Voice. F. B. Meyer was the leading conference speaker of his day. The time came when a younger man, Campbell Morgan, superseded him in popularity as a teacher. For a time Meyer wrestled with the pain of seeing his followers turning elsewhere for their spiritual nourishment. To overcome these feelings he hit upon a truly inspired strategy: he resolved to spend as much of his time as he could praying for the success of Campbell's ministry.

I have shared this stunning example of humility in action on numerous occasions, and it never fails to move me. It is the perfect antidote to striving and jealousy.

Long ago, Satan had a problem relating to God. To this day he never ceases trying to disrupt relationships. I have watched with dismay as ministers in a deliverance session have all but come to blows about how to proceed, never realizing the degree to which they were being influenced by the powers they should have been united in dislodging. It is an extreme

example of the strain relationships come under when the
enemy spies a weakness to exploit.[9]

Realistically, the powers of darkness do not have that many
worthwhile targets in a given region to pursue. It is no wonder
they focus their efforts on those who pose the greatest danger.
Don't be surprised, Peter warns, when attacks crowd in on
our health, reputation, doctrine, finances and so on.[10]

Typically, the enemy directs his forces against an individual or family, often using divisive spirits to make full use of
specific information to hurt or malign. Part of the enemy's
strategy is to make us mistake our suspicions for the authentic
voice of God.

Suppose I am getting to know someone who has been
divorced, or who has had some kind of 'history' in the past.
Things are going fine until a Bible verse jumps off the page,
appearing to question their morality, or their motivation. Is
this a Godly warning? Or is it the devil dredging dirt? We
must be so careful. Leaping to wrong conclusions can seriously affect the way we relate to each other.

There have been many splits in the Body of Christ, in
which basically excellent men and women have been driven
from their posts through people heeding strong and distorted
prejudices, and confusing this with the authentic leading of
heaven.

How can we overcome the enemy's implacable spite and
jealousy? By affirming each other! The more we shout for joy
when we see others doing well[11] (and the quicker we are to
pray for those who are not faring so well), the less room we
give the green-eyed monster.

For Reflection and Prayer

If the grass is looking greener on the other side of the fence,
it is time to water your own lawn. (Anon)

'Anger is cruel, and fury overwhelming, but who can stand
before jealousy?'[12] Jealousy lies at the root of every character
defect. It injects its poison, turns us in on ourselves, and
paralyzes our love and generosity.

There is only one letter difference between the words to 'resent' and to 'repent' – but all the difference in the world in their outworking.

Lord, when I see someone
who is much more obviously blessed than I am,
let me not to feel rejected or passed over.
I hand every pang of jealousy and envy to You.
Show me any bitter roots
that are operating in my heart.
Uproot all jealousy or judgment,
and enable me to bless the people, institutions and
fellowships I have been feeling so ambiguous towards.
In Jesus' name, Amen.

Listening that complements and compliments

Jesus, lover of our souls,
Let our earthly loves be true.
As I draw near to my beloved,
May I draw still nearer You.
Jesus, we welcome You
into the heart of our homes and friendships.
Let common wit and purpose spur us on:
Let nothing come between our love.

Have you noticed how the Lord often 'balances' people who are particularly gifted in hearing the Still Small Voice by placing them in a safe and solid context?

I can see in memory the man who founded a beautiful retreat center, that lies high in the hills of Pembrokeshire. I see him sitting at his desk by the window, working his way doggedly through huge administrative piles. His attention to detail perfectly complemented (although it may have occasionally irritated) his more spiritually 'sensitive' wife, who brought so many precious words from the Lord to the guests who were staying with them. The ministry needed both sets of skills.

You can probably think of a number of marriage and pastoral teams that the Lord 'counterbalances' in such ways. If both partners were too mystically inclined, the chances are that they would embark on all manner of schemes and ideas, and end up like Icarus – straying so close to the sun that they melt their wings, and crash back to Terra Firma. If both were too stolidly 'earthly,' however, they might lack the vision and initiative to attempt the things the Lord had in mind for them.

The Lord balances our giftings, therefore, and makes them complementary rather than competitive. This is wonderful – provided that everyone realizes what is going on. Otherwise spiritually minded giants might be inclined to grumble, 'Why can't they be more spiritual?' leaving people whose feet are more firmly planted on the ground feeling like spiritual pygmies.

Over the years I have probably heard from the Lord more often than Ros – although at key moments, and on on certain issues, the reverse has undoubtedly been the case. One of Ros's most precious roles is to weigh and balance the words that I hear, and to keep me on course when I try to implement them prematurely, or lose confidence in them altogether.

For Reflection and Prayer

I love Paul's masterly understatement, when he warns that we are not wise when we compare ourselves with one another.[13] Such comparisons stem only from pride, if we think we are better than them, or from shame and despondency if we feel we are inferior. Neither attitude is of the slightest help in discerning the Still Small Voice.

Since everything God gives is for the benefit of the whole Body, the following questions probe our heart's leaning, whilst at the same time pointing us in a better direction:

i) How proactive am I in praying for people and ministries I am not instinctively drawn towards?

ii) Do I shout for joy when I see someone else victorious?

Respect the boundaries

Stop – Look – Listen. (Road Safety Slogan)

A few miles from where we live, extensive sectors of Dartmoor are used as live firing ranges for the army. Red flags fly to show when these are 'forbidden zones.' In much the same way, the Lord find ways to alert us when we are in danger of crossing into dangerous territory. It is up to us to heed the warnings.

If we cross the boundaries of propriety (whether in terms of sexuality, or in observing national and spiritual laws), we cannot but experience serious consequences. It is not so much that we break God's laws as that they break us.

I can only plead with you to heed the slogan above: 'Stop. Look. Listen.' Acting on the promptings the Lord gives through His Still Small Voice can prevent an ocean of regrets later on.

Rick Renner describes a time when the Spirit prompted him not to go to a particular meeting. Because he had come a long way to attend it, however, he felt justified in overruling his persistent warning nudges. When he returned to his hotel room, he found it ransacked, with everything of value missing.[14]

The Lord is prepared to share many insights with us, but we must be careful not to pry into areas the Lord has no intention of speaking about. To return to the Narnia stories that mean so much to so many, Aslan rebukes Lucy on one occasion for eavesdropping on two friends who had been talking about her. At the same time he reassures her concerning the friend who had been talking about her in such a dismissive way.

'You have misjudged your friend. She is weak, but she loves you. She was afraid of the older girl, and said what she does not mean.'[15]

Having overheard something she had no right to be privy to, Lucy is worried that she may have spoilt the relationship forever. We have no doubt seen the Lord turn many such situations round through repentance and prayer, but Aslan takes the opportunity to outline a principle we all do well to bear in mind: 'That is someone else's story. No one is ever told what *would* have happened.'

To stray into 'someone else's story' is to enter realms of divination that we are not permitted to explore.[16]

What happens if we allow no-go areas to develop in our lives? We are likely to find the Still Small Voice growing progressively fainter. Often, this comes about not because of conscious sin but because we have built 'walls' to protect ourselves from being hurt.

As we shall see in the final chapter, we may *need* to put certain 'filters' in place to protect ourselves from information overload. We must be careful, though, that the measures we adopt do not develop into full scale walls that keep the Lord, and other key people, at a distance.

Corrie Ten Boom once asked the Lord why she was no longer hearing the Still Small Voice. He reminded her that she had told Him once that she was willing to go anywhere for Him, so long as it wasn't Germany.

The moment she repented of this 'no go' area, the Lord began to speak to her again. He also opened the door for her to exercise a wonderfully fruitful ministry – in Germany!

For Reflection and Prayer

As we evaluate our attempts to listen, we will often find that our interpretation of events turns out to be too narrowly subjective. When hard things happen to 'bad' men, we automatically assume them to be the judgment of God. When similar things befall good people, we rush to put all the blame on the devil. That may by no means be *all* that is going on in a situation.

> *Lord, many of Your ways are past finding out;*
> *yet You are willing to share so much with us.*
> *As we heed the words and whispers You send our way,*
> *help us to respect proper boundaries,*
> *and to avoid over simplistic interpretations.*

Be like the angels! (Mark 12:25; Luke 20:36)

Behold, I will create new heavens and a new earth.
(Isaiah 65:17)

The whole of history is leading up to the moment when the Lord Jesus returns to make all things new. In the age to come, Jesus says that we will be like His messengers – the angels.

What do angels spend the greater part of their time doing? They come *in* to the throne room to worship the Lamb, and then they go *out* on specific assignments for Him. Since our future state will include service *for* God, and fellowship *with* Him, it makes sense to get in training now!

Lord, may we be like the angels:
pure and single minded in our devotion,
but quick to recognize when You call us
to some new assignment.
In Jesus' name, Amen.

References

1. Philippians 1:19-20
2. 2 Chronicles 18:7; 17
3. Exodus 33:19
4. Ray Mears *The Real Heroes of Telemark* (Coronet Books)
5. Luke 5:17
6. Luke 24:13-32
7. C.S. Lewis *The Horse and his Boy* (Harper Collins).
8. Mark 4:38
9. We will avoid many mistakes, and much discomfiture, if we learn to think about how our actions will affect the wider Body of Christ.
10. 1 Peter 4:12f
11. Psalm 20:5
12. Proverbs 27:4
13. 2 Corinthianas 10:12
14. Rick Renner *Sparkling Gems from the Greek* (Teach All Nations). We cannot recommend this devotional compilation too highly.
15. C.S. Lewis *The Voyage of the Dawn Treader* (Harper Collins) pp. 123-124.
16. Deuteronomy 29:29

Chapter Three

Encounter His Presence

> Listen to my words: When a prophet of the Lord is among
> you, I reveal myself to him in visions, I speak to him in
> dreams. But this is not true of My servant Moses: he is
> faithful in all My house. With him I speak face to face,
> clearly and not in riddles; he sees the form of the Lord.
> Why then were you not afraid to speak against my servant
> Moses? (Numbers 12:8)

Keen lovers of C. S. Lewis' children's stories might be
tempted to lament the reference to there being 'few
connecting doors left' between our world and the magical
land of Narnia.

The door that really matters, however – between heaven
and earth – in no way closed when the Lord Jesus ascended
back to His Father. Although He would no longer be able to
walk and talk with His disciples in quite the same way, He
promised that He would continue to communicate with them
by His Spirit.

Thousands of years before the Spirit was poured out on all
flesh, the Lord came down in a pillar of cloud in the wilderness to rebuke Aaron and Miriam for their critical attitude.
The passage quoted above shows how highly the Lord rated
Moses. In the process it also reveals at least three different
levels of communication. First, come face-to-face encounters,
then visions and dreams, and finally riddles.[1]

We could perhaps liken these 'direct' and 'indirect' means
of communication to soccer referees awarding direct and
indirect free kicks. In the case of direct free kicks, players
have the chance to drive the ball through the defensive wall

and into the net. If the free kick is an indirect one, the ball has to be passed to someone else before a shot can be attempted.

I love reading accounts of people who have had 'face-to-face' encounters. Extraordinary things always seem to happen to them. Even better if we are able to spend time with them – we are more than likely to 'catch' something of their anointing and authority!

My mind goes back to the godly Building Society manager the Lord told us to approach for our first mortgage application. He turned out to be a man who walked so closely to the Lord that you could feel the presence of heaven all around as he prayed.

The Lord told him to go ahead with a transaction that many another manager would have balked at: to trust a person who lived 'by faith' to meet his monthly repayments. When we consider all that has developed as the direct result of owning our first property, we can only marvel at how significant that word proved to be.

Many years ago, Ros and I spent a few hours with John and Paula Sandford, whose books are making such a profound impact on so many. As we prayed together, we could feel the Lord's presence 'layers deep' in the room, even before they brought a powerful word that launched us into another phase of our ministry.

Face to face

Show me Your face, let me hear Your voice; for Your voice is sweet, and Your face is lovely. (Song of Songs 2:14)

The veil between heaven and earth is very thin. One evening in Paris in the mid 1970s, I returned home to my lodgings from a midweek Bible study feeling unusually deflated.

For reasons I can no longer recall, my contributions had not been well received. I flopped down onto my knees and poured out my heart to God. Suddenly, I found myself praying an outrageous prayer: that I might be allowed to go to heaven that night. It was not so much that I went to heaven as that heaven came to me. My prayer was abundantly answered as the presence of the Lord flooded into the room. I was utterly caught up in the love of the Lord, surrounded, accepted and *known* in a totally different way to anything I had ever experienced before.

We conversed together in all for three hours. First of all, He called me to be His witness. In the warmth of the Lord's immediate presence, it is easy to hear 'hard' truths. Amongst many pointers to the future, He told me that He did not want me to marry the girl I was engaged to. I had been feeling uneasy about the relationship for some time, but had been reluctant to make the break. Now the Lord was insisting on it.

He also stressed that I should not become a vicar – something that kept me from confusion when people made inevitable suggestions that I 'do it properly and get ordained.'

Towards the end of our time together, the Lord told me that although I would not meet Him again in quite such a dramatic way this side of heaven, His presence would always be with me. When I asked Him how I could be sure in the future that I had not imagined this face-to-face encounter He instructed me to read a passage from Deuteronomy 5:24: *'This day we have seen that a man can live, even if God speaks with him.'*

The Lord eased the pain of losing this intense awareness of heaven by pouring out His Spirit on me, and giving me a gift I had been praying for: the ability to speak in tongues. For several more weeks His presence remained close, allowing me to remain as it were on the heavenward side. This was my 'Mount of Transfiguration' experience, that equipped and strengthened me for all that lay ahead.

For Reflection and Prayer

We do not have to search far in the Bible to find examples of face-to-face encounters, from the Lord calling Abraham and directing Moses, right through to the Lord Jesus speaking to

John on the island of Patmos, where He bequeathed the Church with important insights and end-time scenarios.

Most commonly, the Lord grants these experiences in order to heal, guide, reassure or warn. Ponder examples of face-to-face encounters that you have read about or come across. Pray for God to meet with more and more people in such ways – as in the story below.

God speaks a healing center into being

A certain unbeliever was sitting in his office in Cornwall doing his tax returns when he suddenly found himself writing across the form, 'You shall know my thoughts!' The man, a down to earth Cockney, was pondering what this could mean when an angel appeared in the bay window in a pillar of light.

The angel told him that the Lord wanted to use his house as a Christian healing center. As a result of this encounter, the man began attending the local church, and asked the Lord Jesus into his life. His house, *Hephzibah*, became a healing center, and he himself went on to exercise such a powerful healing ministry that the Church of England commissioned him into the ministry of healing.

A woman saw an advertisement for the work of this ministry at a time when her son had severe health problems. When introduced, this man was miraculously healed, and later went on to acquire the property when the original owner died. The ministry and vision of *Hephzibah* continue to this day in Cornwall.[2]

Of such tales there is no end. It is no part of our brief to try to second-guess God's sovereign workings. 'Why were *these* men chosen for such miraculous experiences?' is not the sort of question that will aid our seeking. What will help is the willingness to turn all our energies – our hopes, our dreams, our triumphs, and disappointments and even our disgraces – into a fervent quest to love and serve the Lord.

Back in the thirteenth century, the stunningly beautiful Margaret of Cortona spent nine years as the mistress of an

Italian 'cavalier.' Outwardly she put on a brazen face, but inwardly she was filled with much disquiet. Her world fell apart altogether when her lover was suddenly assassinated. Distraught beyond words, and laying the blame for this tragic event on herself for having transgressed God's command, she resolved to live henceforth only for the glory of the Lord.

As prodigals are ever wont to do, her first impulse was to return to the perceived security of her family home. She was unable to find the space and grace there, however, that she so desperately needed. (Her father and profoundly uncaring stepmother showed her firmly to the door.) What followed is an illustration of the Biblical promise that *'Though my father and mother forsake me, the Lord will receive me.'*[3]

Sitting beneath a fig tree in total desolation, a host of demons flocked around Margaret, eager to reassure her that she would have no difficulty in finding suitable men to care for her, because she was so beautiful. Above and beyond the deluge of temptation, the Still Small Voice spoke, bidding her to put herself under the care of the Franciscan friars.

Margaret found with the friars the 'parental' support that was so sorely wanting in her natural home. She went on to live a life of exemplary humility. The example may appear extreme, but in our own way many of us can identify with the call to repentance and humility that Margaret lived out, and that Suzanne Pillans spoke of in the opening chapter.

As we have seen, these are the qualities that enable us to withstand the flood tide of Satan's condemnation, and to make an impact for the Lord, without allowing any trace of the attendant glory to lodge in our soul.

Such people, and only such as have yielded themselves completely to the Lord, often experience a special sense of sweetness in their soul as the Spirit draws them near to the One they love. His presence compensates for the troubles they almost invariably also go through, just as His power removes the obstacles in their path.

For Reflection and Prayer

'How can you believe if you accept praise from one another, yet make no effort to obtain the praise that comes from the only God?' (Jesus in John 5:44)

Souls are tested by praise they receive – but they are tested still more stringently when the light of Christ in them is misconstrued by others. Just as many well-intentioned people doubted the Lord Jesus, so there will always be those who misunderstand both our methods and our motives. What a temptation we feel at such times to try to vindicate ourselves.

It is often the most godly who agonize longest over their motivation. The less scrupulous are far too convinced of their own rightness to entertain such hesitations.

We are wise to consider carefully the possibility that we may be mistaken – yet we must not hold back when God has spoken. Since we offer the devil unlimited landing strips for fear and doubt, we should pray the following prayer as often as we need to.

Free us, Lord, from the fear of man!
Make us resolute and incisive when You have spoken,
for this leaves no room for the Doubter to work.

Dreams that heal and seal

Then God said to him in the dream . . . (Genesis 20:6)

If face-to-face encounters are relatively rare occurrences the Lord speaks to us far more frequently at one stage removed by means of dreams, visions and other signs and pointers. These often non-verbal communications get us thinking and moving in a particular direction, but usually require further prayer before we can be sure what the Lord is saying or doing.

To any who may be skeptically minded on the subject of dreams, let me stress how often He does so in the Bible.[4] Every year more and more people in Islamic countries are coming to know the Lord Jesus as a result of receiving dreams about Him.

There is nothing new about this. Back in the fifth century, pirates sailed up the River Clyde and seized a young boy called Patrick. Seven grim years of slavery in Ireland ensued. It was during this time that the Lord drew him back to the faith of his fathers, and set him on fire with love for Himself.

One night, Patrick had a dream, in which he saw how he could cross the country and find a boat. The fact that the Lord had spoken did not mean that things would work out easily. It was only with extreme difficulty that Patrick persuaded the ship's captain to take him on board.

The Lord's purposes for Patrick in the land of his captivity did not come to an end with his escape to France. Some years later, he heard the voice of the Irish people calling him to return. What the Lord began through a rescue dream He continued with this commissioning vision.

Patrick's lifelong mission brought whole tribes to faith, making Ireland a leading Christian nation. In his footsteps, Columba went to Iona, the first of a multitude of Irish Celtic missionaries who set out to evangelize Scotland and the northern islands. Later, from the island outpost of Lindisfarne, they touched almost every part of northern and western Europe by their missionary zeal.

It is sobering to think that this crucial work might never have developed had Patrick dug in his heels and said, 'I don't do countries that treat me badly.' Mercifully, like Paul, he was obedient to the heavenly vision.

Most of our dreams do not lead to such high-powered consequences, of course. They are more like broad strokes of the Father's brush, of which just a few insights and features stand out to direct us towards some particular person, project or understanding. Because our memories are fickle, we are wise if we record the details of dreams we believe may be of spiritual significance as soon as possible after the event.

Shortly after I became a Christian, I began to pray for an old school friend. My clumsy attempts to tell her about the

Lord met with no response, and for the next twelve years, I had no further contact with her. One night, however, I saw her in a dream as a Christian.

To my astonishment I received a letter from her the very next day. Not only had she given her life to the Lord, she had already helped a couple of other people in her village to do the same. I had felt led to pray for one person, but the Lord was already thinking of all the people He would bring to Himself through her!

Dreams often supply a vital *portion* of the guidance we need, but they usually require further clarification before we should accept them as definitive guidance. As I came to the end of seven exciting years in Oxford, I knew the Lord was calling me to resign my post as an evangelist and move on, but I had no idea where He wanted me to go. When I had a dream of black and white houses, however, for some reason I felt convinced that the Lord was speaking about Chester.

The following night, as I was going to sleep, the Lord whispered to me the names of two churches. I happened to be in the region a few weeks later, so I popped in to Chester to pursue the matter. The churches did indeed turn out to exist. They became fruitful bases for the next eight years – but only after the leaders of the principal church confirmed the dream and welcomed me into the leadership.

Beyond these broad brush strokes lie finer ones that focus our attention on particular issues. For example, we may do our best to bury certain memories, but our subconscious is not so easily fooled.[5] Whilst many things *should* be forgotten, we should be particularly alert to themes and symbols that recur regularly in our dreams. The Lord uses them as a discreet way to show us when something is out of balance in our lives.

Other dreams are more like X-rated Gothic films in which the Lord allows us disturbing glimpses into the strategies of hell. Rather than accepting these dire predictions, it is helpful to realize that they are, effectively, a call to pray for the very *opposite* of what we have seen to come about. In other words, the Lord uses our prayers to thwart what the powers of darkness are planning.

One step down from these 'alarm bells' lie dreams that are two parts psychological for one part spiritual. Suppose, for example, that you are organizing a conference, and dream of an empty auditorium. The chances are that this is just the subconscious having a wobble. There again, it may also be the Lord alerting us to the fact that the conference will only fulfill the Lord's objectives if we pray a whole lot harder.

Likewise, we should not be in a hurry to change our ticket if we dream that the plane we are about to catch is going to crash. If such radical action really is required, the Lord will confirm it in other ways. In the meantime, *use* the dream as a stimulus to pray. May the conference we are planning be well attended and successful – and the journey we are going on be both safe and greatly blessed!

For Reflection and Prayer

Father, please speak to us clearly in our dream life.
Help us to harness the pointers that You give –
and to discard irrelevant details.

Visions that inform and direct

Where there is no revelation, the people cast off restraint.
(Proverbs 29:18)

In the verse above, the word *hazon* (often translated 'vision') speaks of direct communication from God to a prophetic people, rather than about people setting their own goals.

One night as I was falling asleep, I saw a girl of student age crying out, 'Lord, I'm so lonely.' I woke up and asked the Lord for details. He supplied me with the address. We went to visit the house the next day, but it was deserted. When we knocked on the door of the neighboring flat – there was the young lady in question, just as I had seen her in the vision – lonely, and ready to hear about the Lord Jesus.

Because our minds are fully conscious when we receive visions from God, there is usually less subliminal clutter to filter out than is the case with dreams. Whether the emphasis is on words, (which we normally associate with 'prophecy') or on pictures ('visions') there is no limit to what the Lord may choose to speak about.

Visions can range from fleeting impressions and steering touches on the screen of our minds to the full-scale trance that Peter experienced on the rooftop – a vision the Lord used to open his eyes to His desire to reach the Gentile world.[6]

What we need then is a different set of skills to know what to do with what the Lord is showing us. Sometimes it is wisest to keep the matter between God and ourselves in prayer until we are sure we know what to do next.

On other occasions we must seize the moment and share what He has given us straight away. Never be afraid to share what the Lord gives you, just because it does not make much sense at the time. The larger picture might be incomplete without your contribution!

For Reflection and Prayer

Lord, we are so grateful for the many times
when You have given people 'living words'
and they have had the courage to pass them on.
(Pause and remember such examples)
Make us open first to hear Your Still Small Voice –
and then to know what to do
with the words and visions that You give.
In Jesus' name, Amen.

Heed God's love nudges

I want to celebrate the way the Still Small Voice impacts the human soul. Words that turn out to be pivotal often originate in gentle whispers that come unheralded, before crystallizing into powerful words that echo across sea and land as if amplified by a megaphone.

When crosswinds blow, the words often appear to fade
from view, yet somehow, like frail saplings, they survive
the storm and emerge to fulfill all the Lord had in mind.

God speaks not only because He wants us to know what is
going on, but because He has already planned solutions for
the dilemmas that we face. Call them 'nudges,' 'words of
knowledge,' or 'prophecies' – may we be constantly open for
the Holy Spirit to sharpen our ability to know things we could
not be aware of without His direct impartation.

I am sure you can testify to many occasions when the
Lord's promptings has opened doors and saved you much
time and expense. Moreover, following one of God's 'love
nudges' often leads to other doors opening.

There are two key principles to bear in mind: 'Consult
before Acting' and 'Obedience precedes Understanding.'

I think of a man who was well into his seventies when the
Lord called him to serve the Church behind the Iron Curtain.
As he approached a border checkpoint on one of his trips,
carrying urgently needed supplies, the Lord told him to move
a package from its hiding place, and to put it somewhere else.
When the border guards came into his van, the only place
they checked was the place where the package had been.

It reminds me of how the Lord showed Elisha in great
detail what the king of Aram was planning to do to Israel. The
information was put to such good use that the king was forced
to conclude he must have a traitor in his midst.[7]

We are not psychic if we hear such things: we are simply
in touch with the Lord who loves to speak to His children. It
is not only about matters of state, therefore, or when someone
is going astray, that the Lord speaks.

On a recent trip to London, I was delighted to find lunch
waiting on the table when I arrived at my hostess's house.
'The Lord told me to have it ready for you,' she explained.
'He said that you are diabetic.' I was doubly grateful: for the
food itself – and for the reassurance that the Lord knows my
need to eat regularly.

I can think of various occasions when we have arrived on people's doorsteps having felt a clear check *against* telephoning them first to see if they were free. Since the people only returned home minutes before we arrived, we would have assumed that they were out – and something precious or important would have been missed. (This is not to make a 'doctrine' out of not phoning before visiting. It is normally only courteous to do so.)

Likewise, when we were staying with some friends on holiday, we had more or less promised to take them out for a meal one evening, when the Lord told me to stay in instead. At the risk of appearing stingy we stayed put, only to have a most useful time with someone who dropped by later that evening.

If we do not act on some nudges immediately, the opportunity passes by and is gone forever. If we pluck up courage and reach out to the people the Lord directs us to, be sure to make a note of their names and addresses. God can alert us at any time then if He wants us to get in touch with them again.

Occasionally, something is sufficiently important that He will give us a second chance. As a young Christian, I was walking down the Metro one day in Paris when He told me to go up and witness to a beggar lady. I resisted, arguing that it would make me late for church! (We can be very devious sometimes in justifying our disobedience!) As I put my ticket through the barrier, however, it refused to work.

The Lord had been teaching me a lot about how He is often saying something through these sorts of things. Instead of pausing to inquire, however, I went and bought another ticket.

This time it did work, but when the train stopped at the next station the Lord caught up with me – and there was no mistaking the displeasure in His voice. 'I told you to go and talk to that lady,' He said. 'Now get off this train and go and do it!' I made my way back and found the woman still there, crying out for somebody to come and talk to her. I had learned a valuable, if not altogether comfortable, lesson concerning the sovereignty of the Lord.

For Reflection and Prayer

Never underestimate what God can accomplish through even the briefest word. One day, a famous guru was startled to hear the Lord say to him, 'You are not God!' This simple but far-reaching word began the process that led first to his conversion and then to a wide-ranging ministry, alerting young Westerners to the perils of eastern meditation techniques, and to the parallels between them and certain mind-altering drugs.[8]

Seed nudges that lead to long term fruit

On my return to England, I was walking briskly up the High Street one evening, on my way to preach for the first time at a particular church when the Lord told me distinctly to go back and look at my car. It sounded an odd thing to do. I protested that I did not want to be late for the meeting, but the Lord repeated the instruction, so I went back to look at it. Clouds of acrid smoke were billowing into the car through the heating ducts!

Feeling decidedly foolish, I asked the driver of a car that had just pulled up, 'Excuse me, are you an expert at putting out car fires?' To my astonishment, he replied that he was! Taking out a fire extinguisher he promptly saved my vehicle. Was he, perhaps, an angel?

On a recent trip to Dresden, I scheduled an extra day at the end, really just to give the Lord the chance to do the unexpected. After completing my ministry assignments, I heard that the Christian classical musicians in Weimar were meeting on that day, three hours' drive away. Because I had spoken at their inaugural weekend, five years previously, it felt more right to go there than to spend the time with friends in Dresden.

As soon as I arrived, I was introduced to a Canadian opera singer. '*What* did you say your name was?' she exclaimed. To our mutual delight, she turned out to be someone I had led to the Lord twenty-seven years ago in Paris. I had long since lost touch with her – but she had been praying that our paths would cross again!

The years rolled back as we made up for lost time. One October Saturday, when I was spending a year abroad as part of my French degree, I had planned to attend a conference in Paris. For the first and only time in its honorable career, however, my alarm clock failed to go off. By the time I woke up it was too late to bother going, so I decided to pay a visit to a (supposedly retired) vicar, whose name I had been given before going to France. I had no idea that he was pastoring a thriving church, and was most surprised to find him leading an afternoon fellowship meeting.

The vicar invited me to share my testimony. A young Canadian au pair approached me at the end of the meeting, asking me to pray with her to receive the Lord Jesus into her heart. And here she was, all these years later, still going strong in the Lord!

Paris holds a special place in my heart. I returned for a brief visit a year or two later and spoke at an evening fellowship meeting. On the following morning, I felt a nudge to visit an outstanding musician who had participated in the meeting. I trekked across the city, only to find that she was out. I dithered at her door, before shoving a note under her door: 'If ever you are back in the UK, this is my address.'

Three years passed without a word, and then, out of the blue, I heard from her. By now, she was on the committee of the Musicians' Christian Fellowship, and had been praying about whom to invite as the speaker for their annual conference. The Lord impressed on her that she should invite the person who had cared enough to visit her on that occasion three years before, when she had been out.

I wrote back saying that I would have been delighted to accept, but unfortunately had a prior commitment. The following day brought news that I was no longer needed for the other event. I was free to be with the musicians!

I love telling this story, because it illustrates that when God has a purpose in mind, He is both resourceful and determined in bringing it about. I had kicked myself for getting my guidance so badly wrong that day back in Paris – but God knew all along what He intended to bring about through this briefest of contacts.

Many precious friendships and opportunities emerged as the result of that conference, particularly in terms of developing the blend of worship and intercession which we have found to be such an effective way of seeking the Lord for wider issues. Effectively, it marked the beginning of an entirely new phase of our ministry.

I wish I could say I always obeyed the Lord's nudges so successfully. There have been other occasions when I have been far too slow in responding to what God tells me to do.

I came home from church some months ago tired, but aware of a prompting to give someone a ring. 'I'm sure it can wait,' I rationalized, and sat down to watch TV. A few minutes later, I had a blazing row with my son – over the matter of what we were watching!

I will never know how urgently the other person needed me to contact them that night, but at least I would have been out of harm's way, and a most unfortunate confrontation would have been avoided.

For Reflection and Prayer

The Lord always has a reason for speaking to us. Take some time out to consider specific ways the Lord has spoken to you. What fruit has there been as a result?

Line my heart up, Lord, to receive more of Your nudges, and to be quicker to obey them.
In Jesus' name, Amen.

Answers that pose further questions

Let him who walks in the dark, who has no light, trust
in the name of the Lord and rely on his God. (Isaiah
50:10)

Much of our hearing comes when we ask God questions. It
sometimes feels, however, as though He answers our
questions at a tangent – or even sidesteps them altogether.

When Jesus told His country-dwelling disciples that not
one stone of Herod's great Temple would be left on top of
each other, the disciples were puzzled and asked Him what
He meant.[9] Jesus embarked instead on a wide-ranging over-
view of the end times. This was no politician ducking an
awkward question: this was the Lord introducing His future
leaders to themes that would be crucial for the Body of Christ
to grapple with throughout the generations to come.

Remember how your math teachers used to insist that the
working out was as important as the answer? Long ago, in the
golden age of Greek philosophy, Socrates recognized that
people learn best by finding out things for themselves. The
'Socratic' style of teaching asks questions in such a way as to
help people see truth for themselves.

In the course of his intense suffering Job asked God many
hard questions. The Lord wasted no time justifying Himself,
but when He 'shows up' at the end of the book, He asked Job
a harder set of questions. I find it particularly striking how
many times He refers to animals that can be of no possible use
to mankind – indeed, which are often hostile to us.

It is as though the Lord was saying through the questions
He asked, 'Look Job, I made these creatures. You cannot
tame or harness them. You know next to nothing about them,
but they still have their place in My overall scheme of things.'[10]

The Lord often chooses to draw out our understanding
rather than telling us too quickly or too directly how to
proceed or what to believe – just as He asked Philip a seemingly impossible question in John 6:5-6 in order to test him.

For Reflection and Prayer

There is a real need to search out ways of teaching that draw out people's understanding.[11] When we feel as though circumstances are crowding and besetting us on all sides, by all means seek the Lord as to what is going on. He loves it when we ask Him questions – but may them stem more from a desire to be prophetic than from anxiety or fretfulness. Be prepared, too, for Him to ask some in return!

Lord, help me not to become discouraged
when You appear to be slow – reluctant even –
to give straightforward answers.
Thank You that You know exactly what steps to take,
and the right order in which to do them.
Teach me to trust Your character,
even when I cannot discern Your leading.

Understanding 'Dark Speech'

A wise man hears and will increase learning, and a man of understanding shall attain unto wise counsels; to understand a proverb and the interpretation; the words of the wise and their dark sayings. (Proverbs 1:5-6)[12]

'Tell me a story!' This is the cry of children all over the world. Jesus did not come to provide people with the scientific formulae by which His Father created the universe. He came to call sinners to repentance, to heal the sick, to restore the broken hearted . . . and to tell stories. What better medium can there be for conveying truth?

Zefirelli's production of *Jesus of Nazareth* made such an impression on me because of the way he portrayed Jesus telling His parables. These well known stories integrate precious truths about the reality of the heavenly Kingdom with the world his hearers were entirely familiar with. Through them, Jesus showed His Father's concern for everything that is lost: coins, sons and sheep alike. In the process, He opened up a parallel new world to His hearers.

Simply telling them the eternal 'facts of the matter,' for example in a series of theological statements, could never have had the same impact.

Jesus taught the crowds about the Kingdom of Heaven almost exclusively by means of parables, but He explained their meaning afterwards to His disciples. Privately. Parables were thus both a helpful teaching aid and a fulfillment of the Messianic prophecy: 'I will open My mouth in a parable; I will utter dark sayings from of old.'[13]

A parable talks about one subject (such as fish, or a lost sheep) but its real meaning lies elsewhere. We need the key that enables us to understand this type of teaching.

Did you wonder what the reference to 'riddles' in Numbers 12:8 had to do with discerning the Still Small Voice? More, perhaps, than we might imagine. John and Paula Sandford do a splendid job in their books of making sense of the less direct ways in which God speaks to us, which they call 'dark speech,' or 'dark sayings.'[14]

At its simplest, dark speech occurs when we think God is saying one thing to us, only to find out later that He was actually speaking about something rather different. You may well have experienced this already – for example if you felt the Lord telling you to go and visit someone, only to find that they were out. Because you were on the move, you were in the right place to meet someone else. It is clear in retrospect that this was what the Lord intended all along, but it can be puzzling at the time.

Similarly, the Lord does not always rebuke us openly, but allows circumstances to work out in such a way as to bring us to a clearer understanding of a situation, and hence to our need of repentance. The more alert our spirits are, the quicker we will be at picking up on the 'double entendres' the Lord 'encodes' in the words that people (usually quite unwittingly) say to us. He also uses the hard lessons we learn, when we fail to think through consequences ahead of time, and insist on driving through red lights.

Intelligence work consists of painstakingly assembling apparently unrelated pieces of information, rather than of the shoot-outs beloved by the movie makers. We likewise will often have to 'unravel' the different pointers God gives us, in order to make sense of what He is saying. They are pieces of a jigsaw and pointers in a treasure hunt rather than full-page printouts of 'answers from heaven.'

The Hebrew word *chidah* – 'dark speech' or 'dark saying' – literally means a 'knot.' There is nothing second best about indirect speech; it is simply part of the way by which the Lord keeps us humble and dependent. If we knew too much in advance, or could always be sure of hearing correctly, pride would puff us up and lead us astray.

In all this, the Lord wants us to become partners with Him through the discoveries we make on the way. He points our thoughts and prayers in a certain direction, and then looks for us to act on what He is showing us.

Sometimes we strive too hard to find a literal interpretation for some vision or dream we have received when it is the general thrust of the revelation that matters, rather than the specific details. When God gave Paul a vision of a Macedonian man calling to him across the water, it could be argued that the 'man' was actually Lydia! The important thing is that the mission changed direction and headed for Macedonia.[15]

At other times we can become too fixed on what we (mistakenly) believe the Lord has said. A friend rang a couple of months ago, utterly preoccupied with a long-standing feeling that the Lord wanted her to marry a particular man. So far as I could tell, his interest in her appeared to have waned past any reasonable hope of recovery. The impression I had was that she was desperately trying to find some way through the maze to reach the prize of marriage.

Children's puzzles – such as 'Help the frog find its way through the maze to the pond' – are often easier to solve if you start at the opposite end and work your way backwards. I tried doing the same by looking at this from a different angle, urging her to consider not whether God was saying it but what it would be like actually to be *married* to him. She had to admit that on both past and present form, he would *not* be the kind and compassionate person that she needed.

The spell began to unravel. Two months on, she feels free and 'clear' again.

For Reflection and Prayer

*Lord, help us to follow the threads of Your leading
until You pull the strands together
and the fuller picture comes into focus.*

The Gift of Tongues

I would have you all speak with tongues. (1 Cor. 14:5)

The gift of tongues is itself a form of dark speech. We use it to build ourselves up without knowing precisely which mysteries we are proclaiming, or who we are praying for. Let us not take this precious gift for granted![16]

I have known at least three occasions when a tongue has been given in a recognizable language. On several occasions the Lord gave me a series of revelations in a dialect of Farsi, which an Iranian friend was able to translate.

This provided powerful and important confirmation concerning the message the Lord had given me, to share with the wider Body of Christ concerning the grief and anger in God's heart at the way the Church is allowing trivia and syncretism to blunt our cutting edge.[17] As a result, our nations are wide open to many opposing and dangerous spiritual forces. We shall be exploring this message in more detail in the sequel to this volume, *Led by the Spirit.*

On the second occasion, when my daughter was eleven, she prayed for someone in Tanzania, who received a special gift – the ability to speak in English! I shall be referring on page one hundred to the occasion when a friend prayed in an exquisitely beautiful medieval language, and brought precious insights concerning our sojourn in Shetland.

For Reflection and Prayer

Thank You, Lord, for the gift of tongues! May it be used to Your glory. Jackie Pullinger, who has helped so many to receive the gift, recommends that we spend no less than fifteen minutes each day praying in this way, because it helps to release the power and authority of God into our lives.

Myths and symbols

> I saw the Spirit come down from heaven as a dove and remain on Him. (John 1:32)

Long before I consciously opened my heart to the Lord Jesus, I experienced a strong sense of His presence 'knocking on the door of my heart' every time Aslan made an appearance in *The Chronicles of Narnia*. I still do so to this day. These wonderful stories 'work' as well for grown ups as for children.

We have seen that Jesus taught consistently through images. In our utilitarian world, C. S. Lewis reminds us of the power that myths and symbols have to portray the deepest aspects of truth. Many people today have become cut off from this way of learning – although the widespread popularity of symbol-laden fantasy games show that people are seeking to bridge this dimly perceived rift between head and heart.

May the Lord lead us to the reality of our missing symbols: of what it means to be a man, a woman, a family, a friend, a church, and so on.

As we bring as much of ourselves as we can to as much of God as we understand, may He bridge the gap and draw us to particular areas of service. Some will feel called to pray especially for the suffering church, others to take the gospel to remote tribes, still others to address areas of injustice. God may well use specific signs, symbols and pointers to confirm and develop these callings.

It is as unwise to go overboard on the matter of outward signs, as it is to ignore the possibility that the Lord may be speaking through them. People suffering from stiff necks are not automatically stubborn. The Lord spoke recently, however, that one person's damaged spine and incapacitated legs were a sign that He was no longer fulfilling the Lord's plan – which was to share the love of the Head (the Lord Jesus) with the Body (the Church). When he resumed his ministry, his physical problems greatly improved.

I recently invited a friend to be part of the worship group at an event that I knew would appeal to him. He was as surprised as we were when the Lord told him not to come. In the meantime, someone had a vision of him sitting in the middle of a floor strewn with sharp tacks. As he watched, some of the tacks were hammered into the floor, making it possible for him to get out of the room he was stuck in.

My friend could make nothing of the symbolism. He was not aware of any particular needs or problems in his life, but he did know that the Lord had been speaking to him for some time about sending him a partner – and nothing appeared to be happening in that direction.

Meanwhile, the Lord had been preparing a beautiful and anointed widow on the other side of the world! By a remarkable series of leadings, she paid a visit to his community, and recognized him immediately as the one for whom she had been keeping herself pure these many years. Right until the evening before she was due to leave, however, (to her considerable frustration!) my friend continued to act with studious courtesy and extreme reserve.

God had done His bit in preparing the couple's hearts, and in making sure that he would not be out of town at the crucial moment – but he still had to do his part. In a rush of understanding, the vision of the pathway through the tacks returned to his mind.

Now it all made sense. Courage flooded in and he reached out to embrace the lovely lady God had brought into his life. Against the odds, visas were approved and they were free to be married.

For Reflection and Prayer

Experienced wireless operators can recognize people by their 'signature' as they transmit their messages.

Help us, Lord, to recognize the ways in which You use particular signs and symbols to communicate with us.

Midwifery Matters

Where is our listening to be worked out? Often, it will be in the place where we work. Many Christians feel guilty about their work, however, because they are not 'full time' for the Lord. It works the other way round, of course. Many Christian workers feel guilty because they are not doing a regular nine-to-five job. The devil does not miss a trick!

Spiritual distinctions are rarely as clear as I may have made it appear in this chapter. The boundaries between direct and indirect speech are by no means 'carved in stone;' they weave in and out of each other, often hovering between the crystal clear and the highly fragmentary. In this section, in which I shall be giving the briefest of overviews of how the Lord developed Ros's calling as a midwife, we will see God speaking clearly about 'professional' matters.

As she came towards the end of her midwifery training, Rosalind applied for a job in Chester, where I was already living. We were married just two days after her final exams. Towards the end of our honeymoon, I felt a nudge to cut our holiday short. It was just a simple sense in my heart – no big deal, and therefore quite difficult to 'grade.'

Ros and I often play a grading game, whereby we express how clearly we think we have heard something. 'A' grade means 'Please take this seriously. I really think I have heard from the Lord, unless you feel that I'm mistaken.' 'C' or 'D' grade may mean nothing more than 'I have had this passing thought . . .'

There is nothing in the least infallible about this attempt to grade our nudges, but it does help us to convey how seriously we feel we need to take an issue.

Even though we had no 'second strand' to confirm this change of direction, we returned home three days ahead of schedule. There on the doormat was a letter, inviting Ros for an interview the following morning. In the light of the way the Lord subsequently developed her midwifery ministry, we can only marvel at the lengths He went to in order to bring us back in time for that interview. She turned out to be the last midwife from outside the county to be appointed for nearly a decade!

Two years later, Ros laid down her career to have our first-born. When Ruth was nearly a year old, however, the Lord tapped Ros on the shoulder and told her that He still had work for her to do as a midwife. At the same time, He asked me to support her fully in this venture.

From the moment Ros returned to work, it felt entirely different. Midwifery had now become a calling, rather than just a career. Many times she sensed the Lord's prompting to pray with mothers during labor, or just after they had given birth.

Women are more open to God when they experience the miracle of giving birth than perhaps they will ever be at any other moment in their lives – and they never forget 'the mid-wife who cared enough to pray with them.' On at least two occasions, Ros prayed for babies who had stopped breathing. Both began to breathe again, without any ill effects.

In the late 1980's the Lord led us to Shropshire. He confirmed that midwifery would be central to our calling, and when He gave us a house next door to a small maternity unit, we drew the obvious conclusion. We looked forward to Ros working there, and maybe even coming home for lunch. Her application was rejected, however, because she was considered over qualified to work in the unit. In any case, they preferred to appoint people who had trained locally.

The Lord had given us His promise – and we needed the employment. The gap felt acute! It was at this critical juncture that the presence of the Lord came so powerfully on Ros that

she literally shook. There and then He called her to set up as
an independent midwife.

The Lord went to great lengths to open the door to make
this calling a success. For over a decade she became the
James Herriot of the midwifery world, with many a moonlit
delivery up remote farm tracks. It brought her close to many
families who were heavily involved in the New Age and
occult, in a way that could never have happened by more
conventional routes.[18]

On one occasion, Ros was attending a conference on the
west coast of America, at which were present many lesbians
and alternative practitioners. As one particular seminar pro-
gressed, 'The Psychology of Fear in Childbirth,' the atmosphere became heavier and heavier, as more and more horror
stories were told of the devastating effects the litigation-
driven culture is having on American midwives.

It was at this point that the Lord told Ros to take the
microphone and release faith into the meeting. A prolonged
argument ensued, which the Lord won by reminding her that
within a few days she would be on a plane and heading back
to the UK. Ros plucked up courage and did as the Lord had
bidden her. Pandemonium broke out immediately (or was it a
mini revival?) One lady shouted out, 'Why does that woman
refer to God as a man, propping up the male patriarchal
system?' She was subsequently counseled for salvation at the
end of the evening. A prominent birth photographer also gave
her heart to the Lord that day, and was discipled for a year by
one of the Christian midwives.

Several other midwives got to their feet and testified that
the Lord was with them, and how their hands were His hands
to welcome babies into the world. We continued to enjoy
close relationships with American midwives for many years
as the result of Ros having the courage to follow the Lord's
leading.

One of the morals we can draw from this episode is the need
to keep pushing in prayer. Pray Until Something Happens!

References

[1] Although no one can see the Lord's face, He promised that He would cause His goodness to pass in front of Moses. (Exod. 33:19-20)

[2] www.deeperwithgod.org

[3] Psalm 27:10

[4] For a few examples of significant dreams and visions, consider Genesis 15:1ff; 31:24; Acts 11:5ff: 16:9, 18:9; Ezekiel 1-3; 11:1-25 Matthew 1:20-21; Rev. 1:1-2, cf Acts 2:17; 2 Cor. 12:1

[5] Elias Canetti wrote, 'All the things one has forgotten scream for help in dreams.' Freud wrote, 'The interpretation of dreams is the royal road to a knowledge of the unconscious activities of the mind.' It is a shame he knew nothing about the workings of the Holy Spirit!

[6] Acts 10. I love the way the angel tells Cornelius that his prayers and almsgiving have come up as a memorial to the Lord.

[7] 2 Kings 5:25ff. Cf 2 Kings 6:10-12

[8] Dave Hunt *Death of a Guru* (Hodder and Stoughton)

[9] Mark 13:2

[10] Job 38-42

[11] Eg Wolfgang Simson *'Houses that change the world – the return of the house churches.* (Authentic Media) See especially pp. 215-217.

[12]. Cf Psalm 49:3,4. The NKJV translates 'riddles' as 'dark sayings.'

[13] Psalm 78:2

[14] When Paul says, 'Now we see dimly, as in a mirror; but then we shall see face to face,' the word 'dimly' literally means 'in a riddle', or 'in an enigma.' Cf Job 19:26-7; 1 John 3:2; Revelation 22:4; 1 Corinthians 13:12 RSV; Mark 4:33,34. Many 'mysteries' only make sense when we discover the Lord's perspective.

[15] Acts 6:8-15

[16] 1 Corinthians 14:18, 39-40

[17] Syncretism is the attempt to fuse different (and even opposing) beliefs and ideologies under one banner, thus effectively refuting Jesus' teaching that He is the only way to the Father. (John 14:6)

[18] This might be a good opportunity to warn that involvement in occult links of any kind, whether deliberate or not, can lead to 'psychic' hearing rather than the authentic Still Small Voice. All such things need to be brought to the Cross, to die, before the life of the Spirit can flow. All sin and idolatry likewise clouds our hearing. Jack Deere looks at various other specific blockages in *Surprised by the Voice of God* (Kingsway), see especially chapters 16-18.

For Reflection and Prayer

Lord, You love to speak,
even without the need for words.
You listen to our inmost thoughts.
and draw our hearts to stillness.

Guard our hearing, Lord;
for listening is the gateway
to the intimate communion
that both we and You are longing for.

You taught us that the pure in heart are blessed,
for they will see God;
make our soul full of eyes
so that we can see and understand Your ways.

One word from You bestows direction
and kindles hope,
so never stop speaking to us.
Even if You have to say the same things
time and time again –

Even if it is not what we wanted to hear,
may we respond in faith and trust
until all that You purpose is accomplished.

As You show us where to go and what to do,
fill our hearts with a compassion
that mirrors Your own –
and may we take the beauty of Your presence
wherever we go.

Chapter Four

Exploring Silence

When he had finished his meal he went down to the water's edge to drink . . . His solitude became a more persistent element in his consciousness. What had he been brought here to do? . . . It was strange that the utter loneliness through all these hours had not troubled him as much as one night of it on Malacandra. He thought the difference lay in this, that mere chance, or what he took for chance, had turned him adrift in Mars, but here he knew that he was part of a plan. He was no longer unattached, no longer on the outside. (C. S. Lewis)[1]

We have interwoven a number of quotes from C. S. Lewis's *Chronicles of Narnia* throughout this publication, which we hope you will appreciate. The passage above dips our toe into an extract from his science fiction trilogy. As the aptly named Ransom explores the planet to which Maleldil has brought him, his awareness of having been summoned for a purpose enables him to cope with the otherwise unbearably traumatic experience of having to adjust to entirely unfamiliar surroundings.

When Ransom meets the Lady, one of the only two people yet alive on the planet, he discovers that she hears Maleldil (the Lord in our terminology) with the greatest of ease, even as she is speaking with him. It is the most natural thing in her world. This poses particular challenges for Ransom, who, though a devout Christian, is by no means used to living in such a spiritually rarified atmosphere.

That sense of being in Someone's Presence which had descended on him with such unbearable pressure during the very first moments of his conversation with the Lady did not disappear when he had left her. It was, if anything, increased. At first it was almost intolerable. But later on he discovered it was intolerable only at certain moments – at those moments in fact . . . when a man asserts his independence and feels that now at last he's on his own.

When you felt like that, then the very air seemed too crowded to breathe . . . but when you gave in to the thing, gave yourself up to it, there was no burden to be borne. It became not a load but a medium, a sort of splendor, as of eatable, drinkable, breathable gold, which fed and carried you, and not only poured into you but out from you as well.

Taken the wrong way, it suffocated; taken the right way, it made terrestrial life seem, by comparison, a vacuum. At first, of course, the wrong moments occurred pretty often. But like a man who has a wound that hurts him in certain positions, and who gradually learns to avoid those positions, Ransom learned not to make that inner gesture. His day became better and better as the hours passed.[2]

This sense of being led is at the heart of the way the Lord draws us into His purposes as well as into His presence. In this context, the silence that Ransom found so highly charged, and yet so challenging, has a special role to play. Whereas loneliness tears us inwardly apart, spiritual solitude of the kind we are describing here is more a welcome friend rather than a foe to avoid.

If we are deeply in love with someone, we do not need to cast around endlessly in search of fresh things to say or do. We are happy just to be together. It is not so different in our relationship with the Lord. It is a sign of maturity when we can hold this intimate silence together, not only as individuals but also as fellowships.

When our inmost being is crying out to be still, we should regard this neither as a weakness nor a luxury; it is essential if we are to be inwardly restored to the point where we can be in tune with the Still Small Voice. Reading a book, watching a film or puttering around the house and garden serves some purpose, but we sometimes need more concentrated stretches of silence both to avoid burnout and in order to fulfil our calling.

A word of warning is in order at this point. Because silence accentuates the presence of God for those who are used to seeking Him, it magnifies the forces that are uppermost in our heart. For those who are going through emotionally intensive times, fellowship, fun and practical occupations may provide a more balanced diet than trying too hard to plumb the depths of silence.

For most of us, however, the more we persevere with exploring silence, the more familiar we will become with the Still Small Voice – and the more we will discover an inner world that contains as many peaks and troughs, triumphs and struggles as our more conventional spheres of service.

Physically, the majority of us may not be in a position to down tools at will and to go for long walks along the seashore – but we surely can enjoy a silent meal in the company of friends, or arrange to hold extended periods of silence during our fellowship meetings.

A 'silent' meal (or walk) is completely different from one in which we happen not to say anything. Because our focus is on the Lord, and on spiritual things, such things may provide just the right opportunity to reawaken long dormant senses.

Taking this thought a step further, the pace we lead our lives at, and the places we go to meet Him all play their part in making the Still Small Voice more audible in our hearts. Places made holy by people seeking God there; wild expanses, flowing water (yes, showers and baths as well as waterfalls!) all these and more can aid the 'slow interior living' that plays a vital part in our quest for a deeper intimacy with the Lord – and turn empty loneliness to rich solitude.

For Reflection and Prayer

Consider. Which people, places and situations stimulate and refresh you? Conversely, which *hinder* the flow of God's Holy Spirit?

Beyond words: the listening heart

Moved by the Spirit, Simeon went into the temple courts.
(Luke 2:27)

The Lord had promised Simeon that he would not die before he had seen the Lord's Anointed. When Mary and Joseph went up to the Temple with Jesus, the Lord prompted Simeon to be present to witness the fulfilment of this remarkable promise. It is a perfect picture of how the Lord alerts our spirits, without necessarily needing to use words.

All of us 'hear' in more ways than just the audible. Listening for the Still Small Voice is likewise about much more than words alone. You will have experienced times when you have known without a shadow of a doubt what you need to do in a given situation. You may not have 'heard' anything in so many words, but nevertheless, you 'know' – with absolute knowing.

Ros and I have long since learned to read each other's body language. I can tell at once when something is on her mind. What we need then is the grace to respond aright!

Most of us are likewise quick to take the hint when a film producer pans the camera in on some particular person or object. A mobile phone is thrown onto the floor, the camera dwells on it, and we are not in the least surprised when it turns out to be still switched on, allowing a most revealing conversation to be overheard.

Our Heavenly Producer finds many such ways to draw our attention to the people and themes He wants to place on our heart. When we are in tune with the Father's heartbeat, we find it easy to 'see' things, as it were out of the corner of our eye.

The more sensitive we are to the Lord's Force One nudges, the less need He will have to send Force Ten blasts. After all, who places a lead ingot on a finely balanced pair of scales? The slightest pressure should be all that is required to tip us in the right direction.

Late one night, I was tossing on my bed, trying to decide whether to drive out and visit a couple who were on the verge of separating. Suddenly, for no apparent reason, our bedside light flicked on and off three times. I took this as a sign to go. I found the couple awake, arguing . . . and ready to listen. The marriage survived!

For Reflection and Prayer

Father,
Forgive us when we leap to defend ourselves
and use harsh and intolerant words.
You have so much for us to hear and to do,
but our hearts must be very still and quiet.
May we, like Mary, sit at Your feet and learn to listen.
Draw our souls to stillness,
that we may sense where You are beckoning,
and recognize things we would otherwise miss.
In Jesus' name, Amen.

Seizing the key moments

The greatest thing a human soul ever does in the world is to 'see' something, and tell what it saw in a plain way. Hundreds of people can talk for one who can think, but thousands can think for one who can see. To see clearly is poetry, prophecy and religion, all in one. (John Ruskin)

To follow the Lord's leading means catching the key moments as they occur, whether in Christian meetings or in life generally. We need to be both alert and incisive!

Following a particularly anointed message, I had a strong feeling that the only appropriate response was to hold silence – but someone immediately struck up a chorus in the back of the room!

Realizing this was going to dampen the special sense of the Lord's presence, I intervened to close the singing down. I could have taken the easy course of action and done nothing – but only at the cost of grieving both the Holy Spirit and the bulk of the conference delegates.

Many spiritually sensitive Christians feel verbally abused when vigorously berated to 'sing louder.' Their spirits cringe because they know that key moments are being missed, and people are not being given the freedom to flow where the Spirit is leading. Try as they might, they cannot flourish in this mode, because the Spirit within is pointing in some entirely different direction.

The more confident we are in His presence, the easier we will find it to lead others into the Lord's presence. We have found that people are nearly always deeply refreshed and grateful when we facilitate times of silence.

I spoke a few weeks ago on all that Elijah went through before he heard the Still Small Voice in the remote mountain cave. As I drew the teaching to a close, I sensed there were people present who had been through 'fire, wind, storm and earthquake.' People were ready to go deeper, so I held a prolonged period of silence, asking God to speak to each person's heart. From the comeback I have received, a very high percentage of people actually heard God speak to them during that special time.

May the Lord help us to seize the key moments in meetings – and not allow every gap to be filled with songs and other contributions that could perfectly well be held over till later.

For Reflection and Prayer

Some time after the experience on the Mount of Transfiguration, Jesus gathered His disciples together in the upper room for one last meal together.[3]

Even though Jesus knew His betrayer was present, He went from one disciple to the next, washing their feet.

Can you picture the scene? Imagine Him coming to you. He is not bothered if you have got flaky skin; He wants to massage your feet because they are precious to Him.

Can you look trustfully into His eyes and see Him looking into yours? What would you say to Him? What would He say to you?

Sourcing the wells of inspiration

> The world will never starve for wonders, but only for want
> of wonder . . . Because children have abounding vitality
> they want things repeated and unchanged. They say, 'Do it
> again'; and the grown-up person does it again until he is
> nearly dead. For grown-up people are not strong enough to
> exult in monotony. But perhaps God is strong enough.
>
> It is possible that God says every morning, 'Do it again,' to
> the sun; and every evening, 'Do it again,' to the moon. It
> may not be automatic necessity that makes all daisies alike:
> it may be that God makes every daisy separately, but has
> never got tired of making them. It may be that He has the
> eternal appetite of infancy; for we have sinned and grown
> old, and our Father is younger than we are.
>
> (G. K. Chesterton)

When inspiration arrives, it often does so at the most unlikely
times and in the most unusual places. Since we are past
masters at putting things off – and the devil has plenty of
practice at snatching good ideas away – we are wise if we
record precious insights as soon as we can.

Much that the Still Small Voice alerts us to is not so much
'new' knowledge as reminders that help us to apply things we
already know. Buried within our subconscious lies the repos-
itory of all that we have ever read, heard, or experienced, not
to mention the emotions that accompanied them.

At any time, the Lord can remind us of some long forgotten
episode and use it as a pointer to make sense of some situation
that we are going through.

Walking in the Spirit enables us to probe the hidden springs
of inspiration – always provided that our practical preoccupa-
tions and mental horizons are not shrinking and constricting
us. Why should we always read the same sort of books,
follow the same devotional pattern, and visit only people we
feel comfortable with?

To continue Chesterton's theme, may the Lord rekindle
within us the eagerness of a child to learn and discover new

things. Blessed is the one who encourages creative people to develop their gifts, and to venture out beyond the reefs of disappointment and rejection.

For Reflection and Prayer

Lead us, Lord, to this place of intimacy
where creativity flourishes.
As we pull away from our work and cares,
we wait in silence for Your answering touch.

Foiling fantasies

'Alas,' said Aslan, shaking his head, 'Things always work according to their nature. She has won her heart's desire; she has unwearying strength and endless days . . . But length of days with an evil heart is only length of misery and already she begins to know it. All get what they want; they do not always like it.'[4]

Stillness and silence are so conducive to receiving the Lord's insights that it should come as no surprise to find that pursuing them can be a major battle. As surely as stillness requires special sensitivity towards the Lord, so great firmness is needed to cut short unprofitable monologues in our head. Fantasies that project us center-stage reveal our hidden idolatries and nurture insatiable longings, which reality can never match.

Sooner or later, these hidden imbalances are sure to escape beyond the confines of our subconscious, and enter the day-to-day make up of our character.[5]

The devil, who is both crafty and religious, uses extreme isolation as a breeding ground for delusions. Beware any vision that overfeeds the ego, or that will not allow anyone to question its validity.

Beware what you set your heart on for it will be yours, urged the saintly Amy Carmichael. Once people become caught up in unhealthy fixations, they end up attempting to justify the unjustifiable – and resorting to that most effective conversation-stopping excuse: 'God told me to do it!'

All the more reason to take another of Amy's prayers to heart:
'Holy Spirit, think through me till Your ideas are my ideas.'

For Reflection and Prayer

Lord Jesus,
When too many tensions come our way,
teach us when to fight and turn these thoughts for good,
and when to rest in Your

Corral wayward thoughts and wild emotions.
restore our hearts to silence,
expand our hearts to love.

Keep us close to where Your touch draws near,
and to those whom we can help,
but far from evil clutches.
In Jesus' name, Amen.

From seed to fruit: the maturing process

'Does he write? He fain would paint a picture. Does he
paint? He fain would write a poem!'(Browning)

I met a friend unexpectedly one day for lunch in a café.
'Writers,' he mused, pondering my literary efforts. 'Aren't
they the people who spend most of their time making excuses
for not getting on with the job?' Unpalatable though it is to
admit the truth, I have a sneaking feeling that he had it about
right.

Browning knew what he was talking about when he penned
the quote above. Have you never been known to say, 'I'll *just*
wait until I've done this or that, and then I'll start?' Before we
know it, we have waited too long, and missed some blessing.

Listening to the Still Small Voice by no means eliminates
the need for serious hard work. In terms of discipline, my
work as a writer mirrors my other calling, to be a modern day
Levite.[6]

Both callings require considerable discipline. I usually write the first draft of a new book rapidly, as the result of the Still Small Voice inspiring a theme and starting point. Very soon, the process moves beyond the initial creative rush and I am plunged into a seemingly endless sequence of revisions, and even complete rewrites. What a temptation there is then to feel I must be a very poor writer, to spend so long failing to achieve a finished product!

The truth is that there is no magic shortcut to achieving something that will be read with pleasure by others. When I leave off writing, therefore, I make a mental agreement to return to it again shortly. I treat this as a firm commitment, and respect it as a serious priority.

The more I train my spirit to do this, the more I find that I can write, pray, preach, play a musical instrument, compose or do whatever it is that I am called to do with some degree of fluency, no matter where I am geographically, or what I am going through emotionally.

That is the theory at any rate: I am not always so good at it in practice. What I have learned to do is to filter out back-ground noise. More often than not, I can write on trains or on public benches as well as in my office.

Cultivating the habit of consulting the Lord likewise re-quires us to move beyond the need to feel inspired. As someone put it, 'Spirituality without discipline is like a river without banks.' May the Lord grant us the single-mindedness of star-crossed lovers arranging a tryst – and the patience and determination of wild life photographers.

I find the moments after waking are particularly important for receiving steering touches. Before I find myself over-whelmed by the thought of all I have to do today (and all I failed to do yesterday;) before the media bring tidings of the world's woes, and the postman brings the bills that challenge my bank balance (and with it my equilibrium), I want to be open to what the Lord may have to say.[7]

It is here that we face our first and most difficult obstacle. Most of us find strong psychological and spiritual barriers when we seek to listen in this way. Just as many professional musicians experience strong and seemingly inexplicable urges never to pick up their instrument again, it is quite normal for writers to feel that theirs is the most excruciating profession on earth.

Like a restless horse, we must allow our inner resistance to be broken in. How will we advance beyond pointless reverie so long as we remain in bed? Complex and competing calls on our time and resources are hard enough to deal with, but the plaintive whines of our hearts can be still harder. 'It won't really matter if I spend another half hour in bed.'

Actually, it may matter very much. Without discipline and determination, our intimacy with God will remain forever a chance affair; a 'hit' when times are good, but a distant 'miss' when competing attractions come our way.

Then there are the specific demands that different facets of our character make. The part of us which would enjoy a quiet evening at home watching a good film finds itself in direct conflict with the desire to spend time with the Lord. Another part of us is meanwhile chafing over a pile of unfinished chores, even while our social-calendar is bleeping a reminder that we are long overdue a visit to friends or family.

The Still Small Voice helps us to prioritize these contrasting (and often conflicting) impulses. At the risk of repeating myself, let me say again: beware looking for short cuts. Too many ideas and publications are presented before they are really ready to be exposed to a wider public.

It will help us to remember that any form of creative work requires us to operate in two entirely separate modes: first as the Creator and then as the Editor. The secret is to know which mode we are meant to be in at any given time.

In creative mode, I get up early, because that is when my spirit is at its most receptive. (You may function best at the 'owl' end of the day.) Sometimes I just start to write, without trying to think too much. During this initial outpouring, I am simply guided by the ideas and concerns that seem most pressing.

This stream of consciousness increases my output, and reminds me where my heart interests lie. At the very least, I am converting my reveries into the raw material from which I can later shape something of real value. In whatever form the material ends up, it will come across with fresh impact because it has sprung from a living stream.

This is the time to be instinctive rather than over analytical. The time will come soon enough when I will return to the work, not as Creator but as the Editor, who must evaluate what has been written as impersonally as if it had been written by someone else.

At the same time, we should be careful who we share our outline thoughts with. It is not that we are looking for 'yes' men who will rubber stamp our ideas, but we may need to guard ourselves against negative comments that can stall the fragile threads of our creativity – especially if we are particularly sensitive to what people think and say.

Highly critical people often fail to catch genuine visions because their brilliance (or cynicism) makes it hard for them to see beyond our clumsy outline sketches. All too readily they heap so much scorn and good advice on us that we feel like abandoning the project altogether. We simply must not let this happen.

Monitor, therefore, how much you share. 'A good work talked about is a good work spoilt,' warns Vincent de Paul. Laying bare our heart, and waxing lyrical on the themes that are exciting us, can make us feel as though we have accomplished something useful, just because we have enthused about it. In reality, all the work remains to be done.

By contrast, sharing appropriately with friends and mentors, can release insights and resources. It helps us return to our work with fresh perspective and renewed enthusiasm.

The good news is that that what we have shared in this chapter is relevant for all creative projects and for the way we church, minister and set about our daily work!

For Reflection and Prayer

Many people find that one of the most helpful ways to discern the Still Small Voice is to write what Graham Cooke calls a crafted prayer[8] – one to which you devote real love and thought. This is therefore a particularly valuable exercise.

Focus on a person or a situation you are concerned about. Ask the Lord to give you some starter thoughts. As these crystallize, turn them into a prayer.

Once you have done this, you may well find that you can go one stage further. Rewrite the prayer in the first person, as if it were coming directly from the Lord. This may sound somewhat contrived, but many people have found the Lord taking their starting ideas and transforming them into something of real prophetic value. Set some time apart with friends or in a fellowship meeting and try it!

References
[1] C.S. Lewis, *The Cosmic Trilogy, Perelandra* p. 188 (Pan Books) The book is a brilliant and dramatic rerun of the Temptation in the Garden of Eden. On this occasion, the enemy comes in the form of a deceived and demonized physicist, who with enormous skill and persistence launches a series of arguments to try to lure the only woman on the planet into disobeying Maleldil's command, thereby introducing evil into a spiritually pure world.
[2] As above, p. 207
[3] John 13
[4] C.S. Lewis, *The Magician's Nephew* (Harper Collins) p. 162
[5] Paul's teaching in 2 Corinthians 10:3-5 is highly relevant in terms of winning this battle in the mind.
[6] A Levite is someone set apart to minister to the Lord and His people (cf Deuteronomy 18:6-7).
[7] I have borrowed much of the material in this section from my book, *Intimacy and Eternity,* (New Wine Press.) See *For Further Reading.*
[8] Graham Cooke *Crafted Prayer* (Chosen Books)

Chapter Five

The Art of Reflection

Think about what I am saying. The Lord will give you
understanding in all these things.   (2 Timothy 2:7)

It is no fun having your deranged 'employer' throwing spears
at you! On the run from King Saul, David lost the plot and
joined forces with the Philistines. The time came when he
was called upon to fight against his fellow Israelites. It was at
this crucial moment that the commander of the Philistine
army intervened, questionning his loyalty and sending him
away.

It is a supreme example of the Lord's overruling. While he
was away, David's home town was overrun by raiders. His wives
and children were taken away – and, as if that were not enough,
his own men were so desperate that they were speaking of
stoning him.

At this terrible moment, when fear and despair could so
easily have shut out the Still Small Voice, David 'found
strength in the Lord.'[1] No phrase better conveys the depths of
his relationship with the Lord. Here is a man so used to
quieting his soul that he is able to discern God's strategy,
even under such intense pressure.

My mind goes back to a man on a Pacific island, who heard
the Lord telling him to cross the island and leave. He arrived
at the port just in time to catch the last steamer out before the
Japanese invaded the island.

Or the Christians in a town in Denmark during the Second World War who were warned through a prophecy to be out of town on a certain day. It turned out to be very day the Gestapo raided the town. There is nothing theoretical about cultivating the art of reflection.

The Daily Review

Dr Pierson once visited a minister who had been in hospital for six long months. The doctor ventured to suggest that God might have permitted this illness as the only means by which He could cause this busy man to listen more to Him. He had hardly left the hospital before the Lord caught up with him: 'You too have been too active for Me, and have not taken enough time to be occupied with Me.' This experience made such an impression on Dr Pierson that he later wrote:

> I resolved to practice what I preached. At the close of each day, I sit for one hour in the quiet of my study, not to speak to the Lord, but to lay the day's life and work open to the Lord's penetrating gaze and appraisal, and to listen to what He has to say to me.[2]

Even if we cannot devote anything like a whole hour to it, the great benefit of attempting such a review is that it gives us a second chance to ponder the events of the day, and to pick up on the nudges that the Lord has sent our way. We can 'replay' them, as if we were watching them pass before our eyes on a video. Then, as opportunities we have missed, or unkind words that we have uttered come to mind, we can 'press the pause button' and attend to the issues the Lord is highlighting.

As we make time to reflect, words that people have spoken return to our memory. Words of encouragement that confirm we are on the right path; or words of warning that save us from error – half-warnings even, that we might have missed had we been too engrossed in our own affairs.

Many people find keeping a journal aids this process of reflection. Rather than recording just the outward events, it will prove richer if we can include fuller details of how we believe the Lord is leading us. Such reflection enables us to trace patterns and to discern links where before we might have seen only isolated events.

Turning sight into insight

'Daniel, I have come to give you insight and understanding.'
(Daniel 9:22)

The first time I drove up the 'Atlantic highway' on the west coast of Devon, I glimpsed large radar dishes. They reminded me how serious the issue of cyber warfare has become. Dedicated organisations hack into top security computers, passing on highly sensitive information to potentially hostile powers. In the wrong hands, this information could be used not only to replicate weapons systems, but even potentially, to paralyze vital communications systems. Since cyber warfare is sure to play a significant (perhaps a determining) role in any future world conflict, this is an appropriate topic to take up in prayer.

The Lord has many ways of alerting us to things that are on His heart. As I was walking down a cobbled street in a Devonian village a few minutes later, I heard a mother calling her child. I instantly felt prompted to pray for someone of that name. I rang her a few hours later, as I usually try to do when I sense such leadings, and found that there was indeed a pressing reason why the Lord had put her on my heart.

I also find that God uses 'look-alikes' as one of His ways to call me to pray. For a fleeting moment, some passer-by reminds me in a certain profile of someone else I know. I take it as a pointer to pray for the person I am reminded of. On other occasions a certain make or color of a car serves to remind me of someone who drives a similar model.

Do such 'coincidences' really come from God? I find that in perhaps three-quarters of such instances there is an immediate reason why these people have been brought to mind.

More than we realize at the time, our prayers may be paving the way for the Spirit to open something up *for* them

– or to protect them *from* some danger. In any case: how can anything but good come from praying for them?

Even fleeting thoughts may correspond to someone's real need. My car broke down in a motorway service station once, when I was on my way to spend a weekend with some friends, who were following on an hour or two behind me. As they approached the service station, one of them had the thought, 'Perhaps Robert has broken down in there.' Unfortunately, he pushed it aside, and had to drive a long way back later on to pick me up!

The Lord uses not only words but also sights, sounds and even smells to trigger associations that lead to prayer and action – or simply to bring comfort. As I was wheeled into hospital theatre for a rather unpleasant operation, I distinctly smelt the reassuring wood-fire smoke of our favorite cottage in the Lake District.

On another occasion, after hearing a distressing report about someone who means a lot to us, our bedroom was suddenly invaded by the distinct fragrance of lilies, reminding us of the lilies that surround *his* apartment. On these two occasions at least, the Still Small Voice became the Sweet Smelling Fragrance!

Many of the clearest nudges I receive come while I am writing. It is as though the Holy Spirit is alerting me by sending me the equivalent of an e-mail.

A few come with such urgency that I feel the need to drop everything and pray. Normally, I just make a note of them, and resolve to return to them later.

For Reflection and Prayer

I need to be careful not to get so carried away with the fact that the Lord is sharing something with me that I forget to take it up properly later on.

Lord, help us to recognize it is no coincidence when
You bring people to our minds. Help us to remain a
while longer in Your presence, in case You have more
to say to us. In Jesus' name, Amen.

Sharing the Lord's heart

> The real prophets of our day are those who can perceive
> what is happening in modern society, see where it will lead
> us, and give a value judgement upon it . . . We should not
> just absorb facts, but think about their significance.
>
> (Richard Foster)

I was walking past a shopping mall the other day, when I felt
the Lord saying in my heart:

> 'This is a generation that has all but forgotten Me. It has
> everything it wants, but it does not know or honor Me.
> These are the Temples they have made – and they will take
> the consequences.'

Scripture is clear that God judges cities and nations according
to the opportunities they have been given.[3] We in the West
have espoused wrong priorities, and made Mammon more
important than devotion to the Almighty. We have acted as if
any deity were His equal, and as though God's laws were an
impediment to be avoided, rather than a structure on which to
base our society.

With little understanding of the spiritual laws of sowing
and reaping, let alone of God's holiness, more and more
anti-Christian policies are being implemented in western
nations. Combined with the increasingly 'politically correct'
climate that causes people to impose their own self-censor-
ship, these measures constitute a real threat to the distinctive
Christian voice in our nation.

God is raising up many prayer warriors as a shield for our
our prodigal continent, but let us be under no illusion: judgment has already begun, and we need to continue fervent in
prayer and repentance. We are on the thinnest of ice as a
continent.

*Father, we recognize that we entirely merit Your judgment.
We cry out to You that we, who know You, may respond in
such a way that this work of judgment may yet prove redemp-
tive rather than purely destructive – and that You may be
more merciful to us than we deserve. In Jesus' name, Amen.*

Listen for wider issues

I will give you what you asked for! I will give you a wise and understanding mind (1 Kings 3:12)

God is interested in everything that happens, and through His Still Small Voice He interprets matters to us. When Stephen Parker conducted a survey of how believers made their decisions, however, he noted a heavy preponderance of what we might call 'privatized' leadings.[4] None of the people he interviewed mentioned any example of being directed into public, social or political actions. This has nothing to do with the Lord not wanting us to take an active interest or involvement in these fields; it is more a sign that we are in great danger of 'privatizing' the Still Small Voice.

As we seek the Lord's strategy for our lives, our churches and our communities, we may well find ourselves praying for people groups, regions and nations with as much longing as we have for matters closer to home and heart.

Such an attitude worries the powers of darkness, who promptly set out to try to neutralize the danger. They may, for example, try to lull us into believing that we are doing all right as we are. If they can succeed in nurturing complacency, we will see little need to reach out for the *more* that God has in store for us. Alternatively, the enemy reverts to brute force, trying to make us believe that the task we are facing is so far beyond our abilities and resources that we may as well abandon it altogether.

If *that* does not work, they may to fool us into thinking that listening to the Still Small Voice will make us too heavenly minded to be of any earthly use in a technologically complex society.

Let us start by restating something that ought to be self-evident, but which often gets forgotten or ignored, and that is that the Lord *wants* to speak about wider issues. A substantial proportion of our ministry has been spent in providing informed intercessory insights to help people pray about world events. We have directed people's focus far and wide – not because any one person or group could possibly respond to all the information we send out, but rather on the basis that the Lord can, at any moment, 'harness' what they have read, and turn it into heart-felt prayer.[5]

For Reflection and Prayer

As surely as the Bible teacher waits on the Lord
to discover what passage of Scripture to expound,
so may we listen to You, Father,
about the things we are involved in –
and about the things that are happening in our day.
We lift to You now especially . . .

Spiritual Warfare

The more we develop the art of reflection, the more likely we are to discern the specific spiritual influences that are at work in churches, situations and localities.

Wherever Jesus went, He wrestled to set men's souls free from the various miseries that were overwhelming them. He saw in His Spirit the battle that had to be fought against the powers of darkness, and He was fully aware of strongholds embodied in certain people and places.

The warfare was at its most intense in Jerusalem, where the religious leaders had espoused the dangerous assumption that when the Messiah came, *they* would be the ones who would be offered star billing in His Kingdom. How insulted they must have felt by Jesus' declaration that the first would be last, and the last first.

The Scribes and the Pharisees had seen many things that should have melted their hearts – but religious pride had rendered the Still Small Voice inaudible to their ears. That is why they felt nothing but anger and jealousy when people were helped and healed. The Lord was grieved at their hard hearts. He denounced them as hypocrites, and declared that they would be excluded from God's Kingdom purposes. Their critical spirit made it all but impossible for them to acknowledge the Messiah they professed to be waiting for.

In C. S. Lewis' *The Magician's Nephew* Aslan has just sung creation into being, but Digory's reprehensible uncle is as incapable of appreciating the wonder of a new land being born as the Pharisees were of honoring the Lord Jesus.

When the great moment came and the Beasts spoke, he missed the whole point. When the Lion had first begun singing, long ago when it was still quite dark, he had realized that the noise was a song. And he had disliked the song very much. It made him think and feel things he did not want to think and feel. Then, when the sun rose and he saw that the singer was a lion ('only a lion,' as he said to himself), he tried his hardest to make believe that it wasn't singing and never had been singing – only roaring as any lion might in a zoo in our own world. And the longer and more beautifully the Lion sang, the harder Uncle Andrew tried to make himself believe that he could hear nothing but roaring.

Now the trouble about trying to make yourself stupider than you really are is that you very often succeed. Uncle Andrew did. He soon did hear nothing but roaring in Aslan's song. And when at last the Lion spoke and said, 'Narnia awake,' he didn't hear any words: he heard only a snarl. And when the Beasts spoke in answer, he heard only barkings, growlings, bayings and howlings.' [6]

Jesus pronounced serious 'woes' against the Scribes and Pharisees in Matthew 23, because words of love would not have even begun to convey to them the seriousness of their situation. A woe is the opposite of a blessing. It is more like a curse.

Jesus' zeal for His Father's house did not blind Him to the consequences of what He was doing. He knew full well when he knotted a rope and drove the money lenders out of the Temple that, when they had recovered from their humiliation, the religious leaders would pursue Him to death.

Prayerful detective work often reveals patterns of attack or abuse that are, to some degree at least, satanically induced. When we realize what we are really up against, we pray and fight harder. I remember once 'seeing' an imp sitting astride a computer that refused to work. When I commanded it to go, the computer started working again. It was an object lesson in spiritual warfare. As always, discernment is vital. Computers also malfunction when you type in wrong commands!

Something more sinister than mere human differences are often at work when Christians fall out with one another. The devil loves to stir people up to bring false accusations against godly men and women. Paul prayed that he, along with other leaders, might be protected from evil[7] because he knew how easy it is for Satan to outwit believers.

Evil is not an intellectual problem; it is a spiritual one. For us, as for Jesus, a major part of our work is not just helping to set individual people free in their walk with the Lord, but involving ourselves in the fight against systematic evil.

Paul recognized the activities of demons within human structures, but he did not make the mistake of confusing social institutions with the demonic powers themselves.

Tom Marshall has seriously helpful things to say about integrating faith, spiritual warfare and our place of work.[8] He points out that corporations are not of themselves either evil or godly; it is the decisions they make, and the influences that are brought to bear on them which bring businesses, governments and churches under Godly or demonic spheres of influence.

As we set out to serve the Lord in these institutions, we will inevitably come up against prejudices and vested interests. Spiritual opposition then is all but inevitable. This is why it is important to prepare carefully for the task ahead.

Just as Paul mobilized people to pray for him,[9] so we must set up networks of communication, involving people who have a heart to see God glorified in these places and organizations.

May the Lord use all who are seeking to make an impact for Him in institutions. Why not lift such people before the Lord now?

For Reflection and Prayer
Help me to overcome evil, Lord –
not just by avoiding infringing specific laws,
but by honestly facing the things I need to face.
May no pressures from within or without
blunt my zeal for serving You.
May truth, humility and love
keep me from the evil one.
In Jesus' name, Amen.

Weighted questions change our angle of approach

He who sacrifices thank-offerings honors Me, and prepares
the way so that I may show him the salvation of God.
(Psalm 50:23)

When I look through the viewfinder of my camera, I
sometimes sense that the balance of a picture does not look
quite right. If I move a short distance and try another angle, it
often lines up better.

It is rather like this in prayer. If we are not getting through
on one track, it may be time to change the angle of our
praying. Suppose that you have been praying for a long time
for someone (or something) that is very dear to your heart.
With the passing of time, such prayer can easily become less
a matter of dynamic faith than of merely expressing our
wishes – vocalizing our unbelief even.

Instead of coming in from 'underneath' what is clearly a
protracted problem, try praying something like this: 'Lord,
thank You that You are far more concerned than I could ever
be for . . . Even now You are looking for the best way to
answer all these years of prayer. Thank You!'

Such an injection of gratitude refreshes our spirit, and
restores us to an attitude of faith. What happens, though,
when we feel as though we are getting no answer to questions
that need answers, such as, 'Lord should I do such and such
today?' Try taking the most sensible way forward and pray-

ing something like, 'OK, Lord, I'm planning to do this – is there any reason why I should *not* go ahead and do it?'

'Weighting' questions in this way often breaks the logjam, and gets us moving again. After all, the Lord has promised that we will hear a voice behind us if we are in danger of going off course.[10]

We may also fare much better if we approach God by looking up to Him in praise and worship, rather than down at our faults and difficulties. Otherwise we may find ourselves getting stuck at confessing our failings and bewailing our predicaments – whether they be real or imaginary ones.

That is what looking *away* unto Jesus is all about. The other day, as I was confessing for the umpteenth time, the particular way in which I felt I had failed someone, the Lord cut across my muttering and told me to stop repenting. 'Stop repenting, Lord? But surely repentance is the key to going deeper with You?'

'It is, but there is a fine line between repentance and remorse – and you are in danger of stepping over it. Don't you believe 1 John 1:9? If you keep on asking for forgiveness, instead of receiving it, all you are doing is expressing your unbelief. That just does the devil's work for him. By the way, it is all but impossible to resent people you are praying for!'

For Reflection and Prayer

Remorse does nothing to lift our spirits, let alone to bless anyone else. In the example I quoted above, the Lord went on to say, 'Step out and *bless* the people you feel you have failed.' Does that ring bells for you? Go ahead and try it.

Overcoming disappointment

I have noticed that many with an undoubted ability to hear the Still Small Voice never seem to develop the gift very far. Many become discouraged by the setbacks and crushings that come their way.

A well-known leader challenged a friend of ours, who has a distinct prophetic edge, 'How do you *know* the Lord speaks to you?' Whatever the motive for asking the question, its effect was devastating, causing overwhelming doubts about my friend's relationship with the Lord to set in – even to the point where she all but lost the desire just to sit and ask Him what He was doing.

Sensing that there was more to this than one isolated challenge, I dug deeper, and discovered a recurring pattern. When she was a teenager, she had begun to exercise a powerful healing ministry. Her best friend pleaded with her to stop doing something so intensely embarrassing. As happens all too often, fear of man won the day, and this precious ministry ground to an immediate halt.

The Lord prompted me next to ask about her birth. It turned out to have been traumatic and life-threatening. The physical squeezing mirrored the spiritual clampdown, and gave us a key to pray for fresh release.

If the enemy can succeed in denting our trust, it follows that we will hold back from using the authority the Lord has invested in us. Effectively, this relegates us to the spiritual sidelines. Trust and confidence are therefore central battlegrounds. Once disappointment finds a lodging in our heart, it plays a persistent refrain: 'I've been here before; it didn't work then, so what's the point of trying again?'

Disappointment is like a leak dripping through the roof. It seeps into our attic, where it strengthens into full-blown discouragement. Now decidedly polluted, the water seeps through the ceiling, and drips into the living spaces of our heart in various noxious and malodorous forms, promoting festering conditions such as self-pity, envy, bitterness, fear – and touchiness.

Every one of these deadly foes is a leak that needs attention. Fail to take action, and these foul waters will pass through yet another floor until they become a stinking stagnant pool that floods the basement of our lives with their monstrous effluent: despair and cynicism.

This graphic image shows us just how important it is to give the Lord our hurts and disappointments at an earlier stage, before these mega foes of faith set in. Once they have established a base in our hearts, we need a major operation to get living water flowing again, and to remove the polluted water.

What will it take to restore our cutting edge? Usually the ministry of others, combined with proactive faith on our part, and a willingness to forgive those who have dented our confidence.

For Reflection and Prayer

Lord, when we, like the disciples, come down
from mountain top experiences, and are unable
to move mountains into the sea or set the epileptic free,
may we yield no foothold to discouragement.
God of the Breakthrough,
we keep pursuing You;
turn these present disappointments . . .
into Your holy appointments,
In Jesus' name, Amen.

When visions fade from view

The Lord usually gives a 'starter' promise at the outset of some project or vision. Somewhere along the way, this almost invariably fades from view. This is when our faith is tested.

Gaining the Lord's perspective requires persistence. When visions fade from view, our attempts to reflect on what is happening may feel alarmingly like a merry-go-round. We go over and over matters in our heads until it feels as though we are going in circles – rather like driving round and round Hyde Park Corner in London, until we begin to wonder if we are going to run out of gas. It is a great relief when we finally spot the direction sign we were searching for, and are free to continue the journey.

At a time when I was searching for a Personal Assistant, Sally Mowbray wrote to me out of the blue, offering her services. Not feeling anything either way, but realizing that it must have taken a lot of courage for her to write, Ros and I decided to go and visit her to see what the Lord might have in store.

Unbeknownst to us, a friend rang Sally just before we arrived to tell her that this was going to be a highly significant encounter. It quickly became abundantly obvious that this was entirely a 'God-thing' – and so it has proved to be. We are so grateful.

For Reflection and Prayer

In the English Lake District, I was intrigued to see a stream whose waters suddenly vanished underground, leaving an empty rock-strewn bed continuing down the mountainside. Geographers call this phenomenon a swallow hole. Don't panic if something similar happens to you spiritually. Stay true to the course the Lord has set you on. Push through the obstacles. Explore the possibilities. Leave no stone unturned. The waters will resurface further downstream!

Father, forgive us when say that You have left us,
and speak and act as though our trials are too great
when, in reality, it is our trust which is too small.
Help us to embrace the royal road of repentance
and the gritty road of perseverance –
for somewhere along these paths
Your purposes will re-emerge and triumph.

Changing course when course changes are called for

Paul and his companions traveled throughout the region of Phrygia and Galatia, having been kept by the Holy Spirit from preaching the word in the province of Asia. When they came to the border of Mysia, they tried to enter Bithynia, but the Spirit of Jesus would not allow them to.

(Acts 16:6)

When the captain of a ship contacts the engine room for a change of course, he expects his orders to be obeyed immediately. We must be equally as alert to heed our Captain's orders – especially if He indicates that a change of course is called for.

Never one to make his plans lightly, Paul must have had excellent reasons for wanting to go to Bithynia – but it was not to be. By ways we are not informed about, the Spirit of the Lord intervened to prevent him from doing so. All that matters is that the apostles obeyed the warning, and headed right away from the region they had been hoping to evangelize.

On another occasion Paul announced that he intended to go on a mission to Spain.[11] As it turned out, he ended his days in captivity, a long way from either Spain or Jerusalem. Did Paul rattle his chains and bemoan how unfair it was that the Lord had set Peter free from prison while his own life was being poured out like a drink offering?

Not a bit of it. Refusing all trace of self-pity, Paul turned his prison experience to his advantage by penning the Epistles that today, along with the Gospels, form the backbone of the New Testament. How many millions have his letters reached? Countless more than would have been the case had he achieved his original goal and preached the gospel in the Iberian Peninsula.

When the unexpected happens, and our plans are over-turned, may we be flexible enough to hear the Still Small Voice telling us to try something different.

For Reflection and Prayer

Let's face the fact, folks. Not all our hopes and dreams will be fulfilled. Reflect on some of the opportunities the Lord has *not* allowed to come your way. Eight times out of ten, you can probably look back and realize what a good thing it was that those particular doors did not open up. If God had granted you what you thought you wanted so badly at the time, it might have prevented you from getting to the 'somewhere else' He had in mind for you. Or it might have been too much

for you to bear. And the other times? That is where we have
to leave it all with the Lord. He is so much wiser than we are!

Father, in every time of change,
keep us alert and ready.
At every cross roads on the way,
be our sign-post, guide and Comforter.
When doors slam shut in our faces,
grant us not just a passive resignation
but an active expectation that You can bring about
something still richer by opening other doors instead.

Hearing 'beyond' our traditions

Nobody is big enough to carry a cross and a prejudice! One
of the best ways to pinpoint our prejudices is to ask someone who knows us well to highlight what they have noticed.

In this section we are asking the Lord to hioghlight our
limitations, and to take us beyond them. All that God says and
does will be in line with His will as it is revealed in Scripture,
but our understanding of His Word may be more blinkered
than we realize as a result of our doctrinal upbringing and past
experience. From time to time the Lord pushes these
boundaries.

Rising from the dead, ascending into heaven, pouring out
the Holy Spirit – right until the end Jesus kept surprising His
disciples into confronting their prejudices. Left to themselves, they would have repelled the woman with the flow of
blood, scattered the milling children, and sent the lepers (the
great untouchables) packing – to say nothing of withholding
the gospel from the Gentile world.

It is worth reflecting on what might never have happened
to the Church had Paul not had the courage to stand up to
Peter. He pleaded with the leaders of the Jerusalem Church to
look beyond their Jewish traditions and embrace God's call
to the wider world.[12] Through the centuries, countless
churches and denominations have parroted the argument that

certain gifts were 'for the early Church only.' Ross Patterson describes how the otherwise godly Bishop Ryland rebuked the young William Carey, telling him that if the Lord really did intend to convert the heathen, He would do it without involving us.[13]

How grateful we can be that Carey did not allow the bishop's tirade to squash his missionary heart. Carey's motto *'Expect great things from God'* kept him going through the setbacks and obstacles – and his pioneering work in India paved the way for a host of subsequent overseas missions.

In our day, it sounds strange to believe that anyone could equate the 'Great Commission' as being 'for the first disciples only' – until, that is, we remember all the voices that continue to urge us to desist from any form of missionary endeavor. In the name of tolerance we are exhorted to respect other faiths, even to the point of watering down Jesus' call to take the gospel to the ends of the earth. May we be as resistant to these siren calls as William Carey was – and as open to receive the Lord's true directives.

For Reflection and Prayer

Enlarge the scope of our listening, Father.
May the Holy Spirit direct our thinking,
rather than our minds quenching Your Spirit.
May neither fear nor prejudice hold us back
from seeking Your face and following Your leading.
In Jesus' name, Amen.

Thinking laterally

Ros and I often say to each other when watching the news, 'What isn't being said?'

The Lord's leading will cause us to explore themes and to go to places that matter profoundly to the Lord, but which merit little or no mention in Church or media circles. At other times we may sense that what we are reading or watching is being slanted in a particular direction. Rather than simply responding to what is being served up for us, the Lord may want to show us a different way to pray about that particular situation.

I am about to give the draft manuscript of this book to a few friends to read through. It will be relatively easy for them to spot the spelling mistakes, and perhaps to take issue with particular points. It is asking rather more of them to notice things that I have *not* included that might have made it more punchy. May the Lord help us to think outside the box!

In step with the Spirit

> Since we live by the Spirit, let us keep in step with the Spirit. (Galatians 5:25)

When I was a young Christian worker in Oxford, I used to visit a remarkable old lady. Although she was completely blind, she had the courage to walk along busy streets on her own, right into the city centre. 'I put my hand in the hand of the Lord,' she declared, 'and off we go together!' How about that for an example of keeping in step with the Spirit?

Some thirty years ago, I prayed for someone in great need. Just after I had read aloud some wonderful verses from Hosea, she received a powerful infilling of the Holy Spirit. With the enthusiasm of the convert, I dragged a friend round the following evening, told him how wonderful it was to be filled with the Spirit, and duly read aloud those same verses.

Precisely nothing happened. I was out of step with the Spirit for the simple reason that there is no such thing as a formula for going deeper with the Lord. Just as David waited on the Lord to receive His strategy for each new battle, so we must seek the Lord's wisdom for every situation that we face.

The strategies that worked well twenty years ago are no longer the best ones to reach today's largely unchurched post-modernist generation, for whom relationships and experience are more important than a top heavy hierarchical approach. Many secular professions are similarly encouraging an enquiry-based approach to learning rather than settling for traditional didactic methods.

This is a vital area to explore, not least because so many believers are left feeling permanently hungry as a result of hearing too many words but seeing too little power Sunday by Sunday. Large swathes of the Church leave excellent men and women cooped up in their seats, with their spiritual wings clipped. More focused support and encouragement could empower these people to go out and accomplish marvels.[14]

I am increasingly comfortable using the word 'church' as a verb rather than just a noun. Whilst the Protestant reformation restored vital doctrines, it did little to permanently alter the way church services and structures operated. Luther may have promoted the *priesthood* of all believers, but he lacked the vision to implement the *ministry* of all believers.

As Paul wrote in Titus 2:14: 'He is purifying for Himself a people that are His very own, eager to do what is good.' One of the ways the Lord can use our ability to hear His voice is to help us contribute to the new, more participatory forms of church that He is developing.

The goals of this 'mega shift' that is occurring are broadly in line with those of previous generations, but the means of expressing and achieving them will be radically different. Young ones are sure to be at the fore, but God will use older ones, like Joshua, to encourage and mentor them.[15] There are few more important things to pray about than passing on the baton to a generation who will go further than we have done.

For Reflection and Prayer

Lord, help us as fellowships and as individuals
to be in tune with Your plans and purposes –
even when You appear to be stepping right off the map.

Yielding that leads to life

What you sow does not come to life unless it dies.
(1 Cor. 15:36)

You may be familiar with the following story. A young minister reached the conclusion that in order to further the ministry that the Lord was developing through him amongst young people, he would need to devote the whole of his life to it. After tendering his resignation in a painful meeting at his denominational headquarters, he and his wife were driving home when they had a serious accident. His wife was flung from the car following a collision and lay lifeless on the side of the road.

Within the space of a few hours this man had lost the two most precious things in his life: his wife and his ministry. At this moment of utter desolation, he heard the voice of the Lord more clearly than he had ever known before. 'Will you still follow Me?' You can almost hear the Lord Jesus asking Peter the same question at a time when many were turning back because the cost of following Him was proving too high.[16]

Like Peter, this servant of the Lord also knew that there was nowhere else for him to turn to, and so he reaffirmed his willingness to follow the Lord, no matter what the cost. It was at this crucial juncture that the Lord spoke a second time, telling him to pray for his wife. A desperate battle ensued, before life began to return into his wife's body.

The man's name is Loren Cunningham. Together with his wife, Darlene, they went on to found *Youth With A Mission*: an organization that has reached countless young people for Christ.[17] If Loren had settled for calling an undertaker and being an early widower, just think of all that would have been lost to the Kingdom. This is why reflection is so important. Are we facing situations we need to 'yield' back to the Lord? Or are we needing to take a stand and not yield an inch?

For Reflection and Prayer

Lord Jesus, we find it hard when You call time on
something that has meant a lot to us.
Like Peter, we want to build booths to prolong the
blessing, and to provide a sense of permanence.
Teach us afresh the grace of yieldedness.
May we experience the truth of Jim Elliot's words:
'he is no fool who loses that which he cannot keep
in order to gain what he cannot lose.'

Listening for enlargement

> Jabez called on the God of Israel saying, 'Oh that You would bless me indeed and enlarge my territory, that Your hand would be with me, and that you would keep me from evil, that I may not cause pain.' So God granted him what he requested. (1 Chronicles 4:10 NKJ)

Almost overnight, millions of Christians have begun praying a hitherto somewhat overlooked passage from the book of Chronicles. It is so entirely appropriate to pray to make an impact for the Kingdom that we could almost say that if we are not praying the 'Prayer of Jabez' then why is this?[18]

Those of us who are wary of the often exaggerated claims of the 'prosperity gospel' may find ourselves veering too far in the opposite direction. There is nothing humble about under performing in order to avoid going over-the-top. To play safe risks turning the Scriptures upside down. 'Reduce the size of your tent' might be a word to an elderly couple to downsize their family home, but the general tenor of Scripture urges us to have faith and extend our service for Him.

For Reflection and Prayer

To realize how wonderful God's promises really are, it can be helpful to turn them upside down. It is nonsense, of course, but if such an exercise helps us to realize how powerful the verses are the 'right way up,' then perhaps it can help to enlarge our vision, and to pray and act with more confidence.

> The Lord is my slave driver, who leaves me short of change. He drives me on by day and night, and drains me of my strength down paths I did not want to take.
>
> (Not Psalm 23:1-3)

Now may the God of all discouragement drain you of all joy and peace as you continue to doubt Him, so that you may end up feeling entirely helpless.

> (Not the Epistle to the Romans 15:13)

Now to Him who is able to do less than we can ask or imagine, due to the lack of power that is at work within us.

> (Not the Epistle to the Ephesians 3:20)

References

[1] 1 Samuel 29:4, 30:6

[2] Dr Pierson was the son-in-law of George Mueller who founded the Bristol orphanages. Mueller's extraordinary faith inspired generations of Christians to trust the promises in God's Word more fully.

[3] Matthew 11:21-24 cf Isaiah 28:21-22. We will look in much greater detail at what the Lord is saying to the nations in *Led by the Spirit.*

[4] Stephen Parker *Led by the Spirit* (Sheffield Academic Press).

[5] You will find opportunities to surf and pray on our web site www.ruachministries.org – especially in the section 'Intercessory Insights.'

[6] C. S . Lewis *The Magician's Nephew* (Harper Collins) pp.116-117

[7] 2 Thessalonians 3:2, 2 Corinthians 2:11

[8] Tom Marshall *Understanding Leadership.* (Sovereign World). See the chapter 'Meet the Corporation.' Writing as both a successful businessman and a church leader, Tom has extremely helpful insights to share concerning both worlds.

[9] Eg Col. 4:3, 1 Thess. 5:25, 2 Thess. 3:1

[10] Isaiah 30:21

[11] Romans 15:24, 28

[12] Galatians 2:11f, Acts 15:1-29

[13] Ross Patterson *The Antioch Factor* (Sovereign World)

[14] David Oliver and James Thwaites outline this problem on page 70 of their book *Church that Works* (Authentic Lifestyle). Wolfgang Simson also explores this new way of learning: see especially his chapter, 'Fathering the next generation' in *'Houses that change the world – the return of the house churches.* (Authentic Media) pp. 257-258. James Rutz has extremely important things to share about making Church more participatory in his ground-breaking publication, *Megashift* (Empowerment Press, Colorado Springs).

[15] See my article, 'The Joshua Generation,' on our web site www.ruachministries.org (Articles and Publications).

[16] John 6:66-68

[17] Loren Cunningham *Winning God's Way* (Front Line Publications)

[18] So named after Bruce Wilkinson's best-selling book *The Prayer of Jabez* (Multnomah, 2000).

Chapter Six

The Power of Discernment

The Lord does not look at the things man looks at. Man
looks at the outward appearance, but the Lord looks at the
heart.   (1 Samuel 16:1, 7-12)

In *The Genesee Diary,* Henri Nouwen describes a type of bird
that fools people into thinking they are injured in order to
draw their attention away from the eggs they have laid in
open sandy places. 'Beautiful!' Nouwen exclaims, 'neurosis
as a weapon! How often I have asked pity for a very unreal
problem in order to pull people's attention away from what I
didn't want them to see!'[1]

Can we honestly say that we have never done something of
the kind? To discerning people, our duplicity is as easy to see
through as when children play hide-and seek. Because they
cover their eyes, they think they cannot be seen, even when
they leave their butts sticking out!

Like Jesus, we are called to a level of discernment that goes
far beyond what we immediately see or hear. In search of
Israel's next king, Samuel sensed the Lord rejecting Jesse's
eminently suitable sons, and persevered until he found David
– outwardly less attractive, perhaps, but the one on whom the
Lord had set His sights.

To discern means 'To perceive or recognize clearly.' Many
Christians claim to be filled with the Holy Spirit, but how
many of us really exercise such discernment? The need is so
pressing that we are going to devote an extended chapter to
considering ways in which we can train and develop this
important gift.

Handling discernment

> We are not called into action every time Goliath shouts, but when God summons us. If Goliath shouts and I come running every time, he'll laugh – and I risk getting my skull cracked. (S.J. Pigott)

When discerning people meet someone, they pick up quickly not just on their hurts and oddities but also on their potential. Their task is then a challenging one. Do they just commit this person's onward journey to the Lord, or do they pause and spend time nurturing them, directing them towards people and material that will develop their latent gifts?

What begins as a personal moment of illumination may quickly pass into the realm of weightier obligations. Perhaps it is this awareness that listening to the Lord may entail further consequences that explains why relatively few ever develop this precious ministry. It is a gift that requires both humility and maturity, not least because the discerning are so quick to pick up on inauthentic words and attitudes.

As we become more familiar with the Lord's heart, and better acquainted with the dynamics of human relationships, we can hardly fail to notice the pride in *this* worship leader, or the 'religious' voice *that* preacher puts on. Not to mention the self-centeredness or uncleanness in another person's life – although we often wrap ourselves in knots in case we are being judgmental as opposed to genuinely discerning.

We must never use our discernment as a weapon to expose, control or belittle anyone – not even to confront them unless God so commands. There is a time for lying low until the Lord shows us to act. There is nothing unusual in the example of a Norwegian friend of mine, who, discerning a controlling spirit in a church leader in Russia, waited until his third trip before challenging him.

There is another reason why discernment does not top the popularity polls. Well aware that even their deepest-laid plans risk being exposed, the powers of darkness subject the spiritually discerning to wave after wave of attacks.

Knowing that frontal attacks lead to spiritual retaliation, they frequently focus their assaults on the areas where we are most gifted. If our strengths and sensitivities can be turned against us, we will be drawn into battles we were never meant to fight, and risk becoming discouraged as a result.

If the Lord is not calling us into action, we may be wiser to pray and hold our peace – like the psychologist in the British sit-com *Fawlty Towers,* who walks straight past the bizarrely behaving hotel manager, firmly declaring, 'I'm off duty!' We must be equally as ready, however, to spring into action when the Lord summons us – and let no fear of man hold us back.

For Reflection

Lord, Your Word says 'snatch others from the fire and save them.' (Jude 1:23) Grant us first discernment, and then the openings to warn or encourage people by Your Spirit. Keep us, too, from coming under the influence of any angry and controlling spirits that are involved in the situation. In Jesus' name, Amen.

Testing words and discernment

Discernment needs to be a corporate rather than a purely private affair.[2]

Back in the seventeenth century, the early Quakers greatly loved and respected the Word of God, but could not accept that the Word itself should always be considered superior to individual leading. Because they were convinced that the Spirit Who had inspired the Scriptures was the same that they possessed, they even suggested that the 'inner light' should test the Word, instead of the other way round.

The Quakers laid a great emphasis on being led by the Spirit, and this produced much lasting spiritual fruit. Unfortunately, it also left the gate open for an ever greater degree of subjectivism. In time, this led to many Quakers entertaining highly unbiblical beliefs and practices. Richard Baxter, the Puritan divine, reacted to some extreme examples by issuing the sternest of warnings:

All sober Christians should be the more cautious of being deceived by their own imaginations. Experience telleth us that most in an age that have pretended to prophesy, or to inspirations or revelations, have been melancholy, crack-brained persons, near to madness, who have proved deluded in the end.[3]

That is going too far, of course. The fact that many 'crack-brained' and downright immoral things have been undertaken in the name of the Lord should cause us to double check our utterances, and our life-direction, but it should not hold us back from seeking to listen to the authentic Still Small Voice.

Within fifteen years or so, the Society of Friends realized that they could not trust the leading of the Light in every Friend as sufficient. Words and leading had to be tested by the corporate will of the group.

For Reflection and Prayer

As we seek to listen to the Still Small Voice today, we face very much the same questions that the early Quakers grappled with. The first question to consider is: 'with whom do we check and test our hearing?'

The second is, 'When we pass on to others what we sincerely hope are inspired suggestions, are we sure that we are not merely transferring onto them the things that we have found 'work' for us? Analogies are helpful, but we should never dump them indiscriminately on others – it leads to a 'hardening of the oughteries!' (ie making people feel they *'ought'* 'to be doing something, as opposed to feeling right about doing them.

Christian tradition – 'what the Church has always believed' – is not something to throw away lightly. Neither should we be so eager to embrace the new and novel that we overlook basic questions: 'Does this word (or manifestation) bring glory to God and Jesus?' 'Are they people of sound mind and behavior, and walking with the Lord?' 'Does it promote unity in the Body of Christ – or does it draw people into someone else's orbit, and incline towards divisiveness?'

Peace – the Umpire

The peace that Christ gives is to guide you in the decisions
you make; for it is to this peace that God has called you
together in the one body.   (Colossians 3:15)

Peace is more the fruit of obedience than a goal in itself.
There is no value in sitting cross-legged on the floor thinking
peaceful thoughts unless we are actively submitting ourselves
to the Prince of Peace.

We considered previously the issue of prioritizing competing calls on our time. The sheer variety of choices we face can
certainly be baffling. As we toggle between myriad television
channels, shop online and venture further afield than ever
before to visit or to vacation, who can deny that pleasures
create their own pressures? May the Still Small Voice not get
drowned out in the process!

To help us evaluate the choices we face, try to sense where
the peace of God is leading. 'In Me you may have peace,'
promised Jesus.[4] The whole of His life demonstrated this
extraordinary ability to be at one with His Father, even in the
midst of endless demands and jostling crowds.

For Reflection and Prayer

Lord of Peace,
make us quick to spot where Your peace is leading –
and deeply uneasy when we are going astray.
We give you now the 'leads' we believe You have given,
and that we are doing our best to follow . . .
Overrule and adjust anything we have got wrong,
and bless all that is of You.
In Jesus' name, Amen.

From Ruach to The Rock: The Shetland Saga

The names of the two houses that we lived in on Shetland
– *Ruach* and *The Rock* – represent the twin poles of our
spirituality. We are called to move in the power of the
Spirit (*Ruach*), but in a way that is constantly undergirded
by the Word of God (*The Rock*).

Towards the end of 2001, an unexpected opportunity arose for us to consider heading north for a sojourn on Shetland. It was not only an unexpected and dramatic summons, but, as it needed to be, a multi-stranded call.

Our first hint that something radical was about to happen came when a couple came to pray with us. They brought us a prophetic word that our lives had been proceeding in one direction, but that we were about to experience a complete change of course. They also warned that we would need to set our faces like flint for it to come about.

We had no idea what this meant. The Lord had gone to such great lengths to give us our present house and ministry that it had never crossed our minds to think that we might one day leave them behind. When Ros discovered that there was an immediate vacancy on Shetland for the post of Senior Clinical Midwife, however, the peace of the Lord came on us, and she felt led to apply for it.

The Lord impressed on us that it would be a sojourn rather than a permanent move, but it represented such a radical move that we felt the need to set a seemingly impossible fleece. We prayed that if the Lord really was in this change of course, He would provide at least one point of continuity by causing our friend Anna, who looked after our two-year old son, to be willing to move to Shetland too.

On the basis that there is nothing to be gained by building castles in the air, we rang Anna straightaway to see how she would feel about such an idea. There was an audible gasp at the other end of the line. To our astonishment, she turned out to have received a call to Shetland herself some years previously! Although she had never breathed a word to us, she had paid several visits to the island and was actively looking for a way to get there.[5]

As I was praying with another friend about what I would do when we got to Shetland, she began to speak in a tongue that I partially understood as a result of having studied ancient languages at university. The Lord spoke of His help in the venture, and of writing illuminated manuscripts during the sojourn.

In due time we sent out a huge number of publications that blended words and photographs of the beautiful Shetland Islands. I found the word 'sojourn' particularly interesting, too. Apart from its primary meaning as a 'stay of unknown duration,' the Latin dictionary I looked it up in said that it could also mean a 'standing still,' a 'post,' a 'residency,' and a 'religious assembly or meeting.' This multi-layered word perfectly encapsulated the heart of my calling: to stand before the Lord in prayer, to send out teaching insights, and to organize an international prayer conference.

Other confirmation flooded in. At one of our regular re-treats, a friend had a picture of an island attached to the mainland of Shetland by a bridge. As if to highlight how closely linked revelations and action are often meant to be, the Lord went on to guide this man to purchase *Ruach,* a wonderful modern house for us to have the use of during our sojourn. Ruach means 'breath, wind or Spirit' of God. We renamed our ministry after it.[6]

We loved Shetland, but it took time to adjust to a lifestyle that was as far removed from our previous twenty years of largely itinerant ministry as the north is from the south. Six or seven months after arriving, we heard about a word that had been given back in 1997, when God had spoken specifically during a meeting of Scandinavian intercessors about a strate-gic conference that would unite Scandinavian and British intercessors in praying for Europe. The word specified that the conference was to be held on Shetland. (This surprising choice makes sense if you turn a map of the north Atlantic upside down. Shetland is the the northern gateway to Europe!)

Back in 2001 we had organized two national days of prayer in the United Kingdom. We quickly realized that the Lord wanted us to take up the baton, and bring this conference to birth. Eventually, *Fire from the North* drew together interces-sors from more than twenty-five different islands and nations.

We knew nothing about all this, however, when we sailed north for Shetland in a violent February gale. As is so often the case when following the Lord's leading, obedience must come first. Understanding follows later.

One year after moving to *Ruach,* the Lord surprised us by calling us to purchase our own house. He showed us clearly the one He had in mind: a large modern building called *The Rock,* that overlooked a stunning voe (fjord). He told both of us the price we should bid for it, but warned that there were other people after the property whom He did not want to acquire it. Months later, we met the couple concerned. They had been planning to develop it as a New Age center. Amazingly, they had bid the same amount for it that we did, minus the small change in our pocket! Once again, the word of the Lord proved true.

Meanwhile, He had not forgotten *Ruach.* The Lord completed the loop when some dear friends felt called to Shetland, and moved into the house just three weeks after we vacated it – and they are making far more creative use of this beautiful house than we could ever have done.

'The Brandle Factor'

> Even in the utmost prosperity, the advice of friends is to be very greatly employed. (Cicero) Do not speak too quickly against things you do not understand. (Anon)

Shortly before we were due to take charge of a lively six-week old collie-spaniel puppy called Brandle, people came to us from all directions warning us that we would find it too hard. After a lot of thought and prayer we decided to go ahead anyway. Fifteen lively years with Brandle brought many hairy moments – in every sense of the word – but much love and comfort too.

Whenever we are on the point of pushing out the boat to attempt something new, we almost invariably receive a barrage of suggestions to take the opposite course of action. We have nicknamed these well intentioned but decidedly discouraging comments 'The Brandle Factor.'

Does the fact that we receive contradictory guidance imply that we should give up consulting others before we take important steps? By no means. Scripture is emphatic that *'For waging war you need guidance, and for victory many advisers.'*[7] It is only realistic, however, to accept the fact that not everyone will agree with us, even when we have heard clearly. The way of the cross sometimes sets us on a course that others – even those we love dearly – will find it difficult to follow us on.

It is a difficult balancing act: to remain open to counsel, without being unduly swayed when the Lord is leading in another direction. On the assumption that it is more important to be on track with the Lord's purposes than to be well-thought of by others, may we, with great humility – and some diffidence – suggest adopting the following principle at such times? *'If the Lord is calling you forward, focus on the Shepherd. If you look over your shoulder to see who is following you, you will get a crick in the neck!*

It helps if we can make allowances for people's upbringing or experience, and realize how it may incline them to reject something as being God's leading. Most of us, after all, have learned to make mental additions or subtractions when reading certain newspapers according to their political leanings.

The pain is much greater when our differences are with like-minded people. Paul must have faced the 'Brandle Factor' in spades when he felt compelled by the Spirit to go to Jerusalem, even though his fellow believers pleaded with him not to do so.[8]

Back in 1996 the Lord showed us that the time had come for us to take possession of the large country house He had been telling us for some time that we would one day live in. After some months of searching, we realized that the only way we were going to be able to buy such a property was to do so jointly with my parents. This was when the Brandle

Factor cut in, with numerous friends warning us not to go ahead on this basis.

The best and kindest way to view apparently contradictory guidance is to realize that people may be glimpsing how difficult certain aspects of a calling may prove to be. That is entirely different, however, from a project being either wrong or doomed to failure. To hold back from following the Spirit's leading just because there will be difficulties along the way is not an option – not least because it would prevent the Lord from fulfilling many of His purposes.

As things turned out, the Lord used our six year sojourn in the house in really special ways – including the hosting of numerous precious retreats – before the call of the Lord whisked us north to Shetland and then, more recently, south to Devon.

For Reflection and Prayer
Lord, help us to tell the difference between Your restraining hand, and people's negative comments!

When the timing is out

'Do not look so sad, Lucy. We shall meet again soon.' 'Please, Aslan,' said Lucy, 'What do you call soon?' 'I call all times soon,' said Aslan, and instantly he was vanished away. (C. S. Lewis)[9]

If there is one issue above all others that causes us problems when it comes to listening to the Lord, it is the matter of timing. Partly this is because the words God speaks to us often have a short, medium and long term application. This is a matter of multiple fulfilments and 'layers.'

It is also perfectly possible to hear something correctly, but to be quite mistaken about when it is going to happen. There is a time and a place for a word to be given, but often an entirely different one for it to be worked out in.

This is hardly surprising when you realize that God's call comes from the heart of eternity. It links into our timescale with perfect precision in its final outworking, but it *originates* in an altogether different time sphere. Because we have received God's leading does not mean that we should automatically act on it there and then.

On page twenty five we hinted that there is often a distinction between a *call* (which gets us thinking and preparing in a particular direction) and a *commission* – that is, the actual moment when we need to take action. Understanding this distinction will cause us to double-check sudden impulses, and save us from acting prematurely. More times than I can count I have said something like, 'I feel we should go and visit x.' Ros has agreed, but balanced my eagerness: 'Sure. But not today!'

We are great advocates of applying the military adage, 'Time spent in reconnaissance is seldom wasted.' It has saved us from numerous costly mistakes. When we first moved into a new house, we needed to replace the aged kitchen units. We saw some we liked in a local store, but felt a check against buying them.

Four months later, we saw the same units somewhere else, but this time with a 50% discount. 'They're the right ones,' the Lord said. 'Don't buy them!' Two months later, the Lord suddenly said, 'Today's the day. Buy them!' For that day only they were being promoted with a 60% reduction.

When the Lord allows a prolonged delay between a call and its outworking, there is always a reason. If the call takes the form of a warning, the Lord often allows an extended period of time between announcing His sentence and actually carrying it out.

This is because He wants to give people the maximum chance possible to repent. Thus we find Jeremiah proclaiming with great urgency (and accuracy) that the Babylonians were coming, but all of forty years before they actually did so.

As we hinted in the last chapter, the Lord does not usually give us a once-and-forever set of guidance that will last us a lifetime. He may well want to fine-tune (or even supersede) the original pattern as events unfold. The principle is simple, even if the practice is challenging: 'Guidance comes as and when we need it.'

How eagerly Mary and Joseph must have received the angel's summons to return to Israel. At last their enforced status as refugees in Egypt was over! When they reached the border, however, they heard the disturbing news that Herod's equally pathological son was now reigning in Jerusalem. Just think what might have happened if they had decided that God had called them back they might as well press on to Bethlehem! Instead, they heeded the warning the Lord sent them in a dream, and headed north to Nazareth.[10]

For Reflection and Prayer

Just as we need maturity to handle the matter of timing, so we also require discernment in the way we appropriate the promises of God. For obvious reasons, many never apply to us – and of those that that do, most are still conditional on our continuing response, rather than being automatically bound to happen.

> *Lord, help us to be in step*
> *with the promises You are giving us,*
> *and the timing of their fulfilment,*
> *for You often give hints today*
> *that You will fulfill many years down the road.*

By many strands

> A matter must be established by the testimony of two or three witnesses. (Deuteronomy 19:15)

Outside Scalloway Harbour in Shetland, three harbour lights (white, green and red) guide sailors along the navigation channel between the cluster of jagged rocks and islands. Only when all three of these lights line up and appear as one white light is it safe to enter the harbour.

Bob Mumford counsels that when God is about to lead us along some major new path, He will normally confirm His word to us in several different ways. He suggests that we should look for at least three of the following strands of guidance to line up before accepting that some direction really does represent the authentic leading of the Still Small Voice: confirmation from the Word, the inner witness of the Spirit, the agreement of other mature Christians, and the specific opening or shutting of doors.[11]

Nearly three and a half years after we moved to Shetland, three people came to us separately to tell us the same thing: that the moment we had completed our assignment – the prayer conference for the northern nations – the Lord would recall us rapidly down south again.

Although this call came earlier than we had expected, we began to seek an exit strategy. The transition proved highly fraught. As we shall be describing in the next chapter, Ros was under intense pressure at work; several promising leads failed to develop, and the enemy did all he could to keep the uncertainties as intense as possible. Friends kept praying. One saw us in a hot air balloon, heading south and landing in a remote and rural region.

The picture strengthened us through the painful and perplexing months. Suddenly, it all happened. A job opened up and we rather miraculously found a house to live in. Less than three weeks after the Conference had finished, we were on the boat and heading south to Devon.

For Reflection and Prayer

Most of the mistakes I have made in matters of guidance have come about as the result of allowing myself to be convinced too easily by one or two strands of guidance, instead of waiting for the Lord to confirm both the details and the timing. Even when some initial piece of guidance seems overwhelmingly strong, we should be wary of acting on one strand alone – especially if it involves major changes.

Fleeces and decision-making

'If You will save Israel by my hand as You have promised, look, I will place a wool fleece on the threshing floor.'
(Judges 6:36-37)

The Lord never intended decision-making to be our responsibility alone. At the same time, we should be cautious of trying to devolve *all* responsibility onto the Lord by laying arbitrary fleeces,[13] such as, 'If such and such happens, then it must be right.' Neither should we try to cut deals with the Lord along the lines that 'if You do *this,* then I will do *that.'*

Although it is arguably acceptable as a Scriptural model to lay fleeces, there is one potential danger. If circumstances *do* line up with the terms laid down in the fleece, we may assume our quest for guidance to be at an end. The fact that Gideon asked for *two* signs suggests it might be wiser to regard fleeces, like other strands, as representing one *part* of the confirmation we are looking for.

How about those occasions when other people bring us 'directive' guidance? We will look in *Led by the Spirit* at how careful we should be about acting on such words. We can recall a number of occasions, however, when people have brought us words that have launched us in entirely new directions – usually when something was too far outside our experience (or faith levels) for us to have thought of it for ourselves.

I am aware that insecure and under-affirmed people can subconsciously use prophecies and revelations as a means of boosting their ego, or even their control over people. It is as though they feel their ability to get words for other people in some way 'proves' their ministry When off-beam prophecies are forcefully presented, rather than lovingly offered, people are left to accept them at face value, or to discard them altogether. This can cause much hurt and confusion, and lead to people who 'see through them' becoming disillusioned with the whole concept of listening.

Perhaps for reasons such as this, Paul Tillich argues in favor of keeping reason and spiritual experiences rigidly apart from each other.[12] I do not agree with him. It is surely a far better sign of how well integrated listening to the Lord is in our lives if we are able to satisfy *both* sets of criteria along the lines of Acts 15:28: 'It seemed good to the Holy Spirit and to us.'

For Reflection and Prayer
Father, help us to know, which decisions are ours,
and which are only Yours to take.

Doors opening: stay inside!

> When I went to Troas to preach the gospel of Christ and
> found that the Lord had opened a door for me, I still had no
> peace of mind, because I did not find my brother Titus there.
> So I said good-bye to them and went on to Macedonia.
>
> (2 Corinthians 2:12-13)

When the elevator stops, the automated voice announces:
'Doors opening' and we duly prepare to step out. Except that
sometimes we may not be meant to get out at this particular
floor. What happens, for example, if you are blessed to have
a whole range of possibilities to choose from? It is patently
not enough to reduce our quest for guidance to waiting to see
whether a particular door opens up, because several already
have – and one is sure to be better than the others.

In the quote above, Paul was clearly experiencing an 'open
door' in Troas. People were hanging onto his words and
paying him well – so why not settle down and enjoy the
luxury limousine? 'Come and hear Pastor Paul' sounds a
decidedly better proposition than 'Go and visit Prisoner
Paul!'

Paul knew, however, that the Lord had called him to work
with Titus. Not finding him there, he forsook the open door
and set off on an obstacle-strewn pilgrimage to Macedonia.[13]

If the Lord has something richer in mind, may we have the
courage not to settle for second best! When I first moved to
the Paris region, I attended a traditional local church. It was
immensely unexciting, but I felt a certain loyalty to it, simply
because it was close by. The time came when I knew I had to
overcome my feelings and venture further afield. The Lord
began immediately to do the most remarkable things. If I had
allowed a false sense of duty to limit me, many wonderful
things would never have happened.

For Reflection and Prayer

Immediately before we embark on a difficult calling, a door may open that appears to offer us an easier course of action. It pays to be careful. Is this door really of God? Since the same word is used in both Greek and Hebrew for 'tempt,' 'test,' and 'try,' there are several possibilities. When the devil is tempting us, the Lord may be testing us, and our souls are being tried. May the Lord give us the courage to choose the highest way forward rather than settling for the 'easiest.'

Discordant voices

> Solid food is for the mature, who by constant use have trained themselves to distinguish good from evil.
>
> (Hebrews 5:14)

Many of the discordant voices that echo in our minds are nothing but the distorted projections of unresolved emotional conflicts, and an immature spirituality that is either over optimistic or underdeveloped. Our unredeemed nature predisposes us to hear what we want to hear – except, of course, perversely, when it inclines us to expect the precise opposite of what it most wants to hear!

Transactional Analysis goes some way to explaining this confusion when it speaks of the immature child voice within us clamoring for attention and approval. This child voice promises great things, but because it has no substance, it shies away from testing and inspection. The delusory promises of the child voice can lead us far astray. It wants all sorts of good things – and preferably right now! It is so deceptive that it even tries to reassure us that the sins of the flesh are perfectly acceptable in the sight of a loving God.

At the opposite end of the spectrum we find the parent voice. Speaking through our distorted conscience, this voice counterfeits the Still Small Voice, and imposes stern demands. At first sight, it may appear formidably 'righteous.' In reality, it owes more to a misguided idea of what religion *ought* to be, rather than to the true freedom of the Holy Spirit.

Following this voice leads to a kill-joy legalism which easily degenerates into a particularly unpleasant form of abuse.

The parent voice establishes 'control' in the hands of people who, deep down, relish the chance to exercise it. It is the power that lies behind totalitarian regimes and cults. Who is most likely to take this spirit on board? Those who are not truly humble, who (quite possibly to compensate for inner inadequacies) are grasping for positions of power.

People who have been used by the Lord in the past are by no means exempt from mistaking the parent voice for the authentic Still Small Voice. Some who were at the forefront of previous moves of God prove unable or unwilling to adjust when the Lord moves on, even to the point where they end up opposing what the Lord is doing.

Almost all new moves of the Spirit contain a measure of excess before swinging back into balance – but those whose spirits have been hardened by the parent voice are too self-righteous, and too judgmental, to make allowances for this.[14]

It is precisely these patterns of control and domination that drive many lovers (or would-be lovers) of Jesus away from Church. Ultimately, the voice of control (the parent voice) represents the way of self and Satan.

The secret formula that satanists are taught at the highest level of their initiation is, 'Let my will be done in everything.' This is the direct antithesis of all we long for when we pray, 'Lord, let *Your* will be in done in everything.'

Sensitivity to the Still Small Voice checks the demands of both the child voice and the parent voice, and sets us free from making unreasonable demands on our long-suffering partners, friends and pastors. When we look to others to fulfill needs that only the Lord can meet, we are as much off-course as when we expect God to do things for which we must accept responsibility.

When people have been taken captive by dominating and controlling 'parent' spirits, they may well need to be set free from the abuse they have suffered. Tragically, leaders in the

Christian community are often amongst those most guilty of crushing others through their strong personalities and harsh words. This is especially the case if they have fallen into the trap of assuming that the means justifies the end in order to fulfill some vision they believe the Lord has given them.

If we have been making unfair requests on our friends, colleagues and (most especially) our spouses, there are steps we need to take to put matters right. We honor the Lord best by loving each other.

For Reflection and Prayer

Here is a very short prayer, but one that may require considerable thought and repentance:

Lord, set me free from the scars of such abuse.
Show me too where I am guilty of controlling others.
Make me one who steers people closer to You,
rather than making them dependent on me.
In Jesus' name, Amen.

Avoiding the trammel net[15]

Listening is linked to opportunity and to action. God speaks not only because He has something to *say* but because there are things He wants us to *do*. You are probably as tired as I am, however, of getting caught in a trammel net as a result of leaping to respond to the expectations that other people place on us.

When a friend of mine moved to a new region, she was beset by invitations to do this and to attend the other. She felt the Lord impressing on her that she must not allow herself to become 'trammeled' into doing things just because they sounded sensible, and because she was gifted in those areas.

The Lord Jesus must have walked straight past many people who were in genuine need. It is flattering to be asked to do things (especially if they pay well!) but wisdom lies in prayerfully assessing the invitations that come our way.

It is not that we are called to be prima donnas who refuse to lend a helping hand, but neither can we afford to pay too little attention to God's highest call on our lives.

Growth in any aspect of life depends on a right structuring of priorities. If we can identify the central goals in our life, we have far more chance of allowing them to direct and govern our lives. Otherwise we will be in danger of 'aiming at nothing and hitting it every time.'

Leaders especially need to take care to follow the Spirit's prompting, rather than allowing people's demands to dominate their schedule. So much depends on their stewardship of time, and on their sensitivity in not imposing unfair expectations on those for whom they have pastoral responsibility.

It is very important for us to choose carefully who we spend our time with. To help us understand the different character-types we rub up against, Gordon MacDonald identifies the following:[16]

VIPs (Very Important People). Wise ones, whose wisdom sharpens our lives, and to whom we look for accountability.

VTPs (Very Trainable People). These are people who are just waiting for someone to light the blue touch paper. We should invest heavily in their lives.

VNPs (Very Nice People). These people make up the majority of church congregations. They would not dream of doing wrong, but they may still be quite some way from the cutting edge.

VDPs (Very Draining People) complete the list. These people are such past masters at draining our time and energies that we can easily end up spending huge quantities of time *almost* helping these people, instead of taking proactive steps to befriend and disciple people we really can help, and be helped by.

The Lord does not want VDPs to impose their will on us and determine our schedule. This is not to write the VDPs off. By God's grace all and any can change, but we may need to reexamine our calendar in the light of this understanding. If

VDPs are 'leeching' our life away, we may need to take more time out to pursue contact with the VIPs who keep watch over us.

At all costs we must not permit the incessant demands of the VDPs to prevent us from reaching out to the strategic VTPs. These people are usually so sensitive to our time pressures that they hold back from approaching us, in case they prove a burden to us. This is a great tragedy. They might have benefited greatly had they had the courage to pursue their desire to reach out to us. If they will not come to us, it is up to us to go out of our way to nurture and encourage them.

For Reflection and Prayer

The following exercise will help you to prioritize your lifestyle in the light of the Lord's leading.

Draw three columns on a sheet of paper. In the first, write down your broad purposes – the themes that God is stressing in your life. If you can, prioritize them in terms of the importance you believe they should have.

In the second column, write down the activities you are currently involved in, as well as some of the things you have been invited to do, or one day hope you may do. It will be quite a mish-mash, but jot down as many as you can think of. Prioritize these, too, in order of the importance you accord them.

Finally, in column three, list all the activities according to how much time you are devoting to each activity.

The results are easy to collate. Notice in particular things that take up a considerable portion of your time and energies but which are not amongst your stated priorities.

Does the way you are spending your time reflect these priorities? If not, what is stopping you from accessing your calling more fully? Is it health, work or family commitments? Or are you simply insufficiently determined to overcome the obstacles?

Checking our track record

'I shall go back to Calormen,' said Bree, his face mournful as only a horse's can be. 'What?' said Aravis, 'back to slavery?' 'Yes,' said Bree. 'Slavery is all I'm fit for. How can I ever show my face among the free Horses of Narnia? . . . I've lost everything.'

'My good horse,' said the Hermit, 'You've lost nothing but your self-conceit.'[17]

The fact that we hear the Lord accurately in one area of our life is immensely encouraging. For every word we hear correctly, however, there remains a 99% iceberg of insights that we are either not privy to, or are hearing less accurately about.

If we are wise, we will check our track record as carefully and as objectively as possible – and learn from our mistakes. As we ponder the things we believe the Lord has said to us, and analyze how accurate they have proved to be, we may see patterns emerging – areas where we hear with considerable confidence, and others where we are far less reliable.

Some of these mistakes may be rather more serious than the 'once-off blips' we would like to dismiss them as. They may be early-warning signs that we are vulnerable to deception in that particular area. Nothing but total honesty (and openness to correction) will help us to recognize where there is some root problem that needs dealing with.

Gun crews employ spotters to mark the fall of shots. They identify when the gunner is over the top (OTT), short of the target, wide of the mark or bang on the bull's eye. OTT listening happens when we confuse faith and presumption. The two run much closer to each other than most people realize, but lead to diametrically opposing outcomes. Most of us stray the wrong side from time to time – but those who are wise are quick to get back on track.

We go wide of the mark when we follow some wrong leading, or fail to embark on some proper course of action. For convenience, we will call this 'error.'

When a Christian lies, steals or lives with his heart set on someone else's wife or husband, how can the flow of God's Spirit not be hindered? Ultimately, there is no such thing as secret sin. What one person does always has implications for the wider Body.

Heresy also takes us wide of the mark, but it differs from error in that it often starts by taking some *true* idea and pushing it too far. Many people persist in pursuing some wrong course of action to the bitter end, hoping against hope for some never-never breakthrough that will lead to a fairy-tale ending.

If the Lord never sanctioned the project, however, all their very considerable efforts will come to naught, and they will merely go further and further off course.

When people are heading wide of the mark, and their error remains unchecked, there is a real danger of sailing right off the spiritual chart and into the blue yonder. Others wake up to what is going on, and make a determined effort to get back on course.

When people become aware that what they had thought was discernment is actually something quite different, every-thing depends on their response.

Some are so shocked at discovering how wide of the mark they have strayed that they lose confidence altogether in seeking the Still Small Voice. For fear of getting it wrong again, they frequently retrench into a supposedly 'safer' form of the faith – and thereby greatly reduce the likelihood of ever taking part in any further Spirit-led adventures.

We are no wiser if we hold back at this stage than if we vow never to get into a car again after an accident. It makes it all but inevitable that we will fall short of targets that, had we been willing to persevere, the Lord would have helped us to achieve.

Where pride holds sway, and denial cuts in, the whole process logjams. Lack of humility can jeopardize everything. Great is the rejoicing in Heaven, however, when error is acknowledged, and sin confessed. Everything is once again possible.

May we be sensitive to the warnings the Holy Spirit sends us! Most often, these will come through His Word and His people.

No wonder David prayed in Psalm 141:5, 'Let a righteous man strike me – it is a kindness; let him rebuke me – it is oil on my head. My head will not refuse it.' Not every rebuke will be justified, but it may contain grains of truth that we need to face.

If we find even helpful criticism hard to accept, is this because we are too proud to admit our mistakes? Or is it because we have such a low opinion of ourselves that we regard any criticism as a threat?

Humility is good, but self-belittling is not. Since the Lord is not writing us out of the script of life, neither must we. Whatever mistakes we have made, the Lord can always pick us up one more time than we can get it wrong!

For Reflection and Prayer

Lord, please show me when I am over the top,
short of the target, or wide of the mark.
Where I have got things wrong,
may I not be too proud
or too stubborn
to retrace my steps,
If I hang on grimly when I am mistaken,
I will not only end up disillusioned myself
but I will spread these seeds of error to others.
So, Lord, I give You my many mistakes.
Help me to learn from them,
and to recognize when I am in danger of repeating them.
May Your grace redeem what I cannot undo,
and turn even My mistakes around for good.
I give You especially the matter of . . .

Putting things right

'This time he found he could look straight into the Lion's eyes. He had forgotten his troubles and felt absolutely content.' (C. S. Lewis)[18]

Someone pointed out a place to me last year in the Faroe Islands that has apparently remained resistant to the fullness of the Holy Spirit. It happened as the result of a group of over zealous believers paying a visit fifty years ago, claiming that they could walk on water between two islands. Their water-logged feet not only made a nonsense of their boast, but created a blockage that has yet to be fully overcome.

Without falling into the pits of condemnation, we need to face the fact that whenever we claim that the Lord has spoken, when in reality He has done nothing of the sort, we risk setting up a stumbling block that others may trip over.

At the same time, John and Paula Sandford remind us in *The Elijah Task* that none of us graduate in the school of listening with our pride intact. God allows even those who are seemingly very mature to fall over from time to time, if only to keep them from taking undue pride in their giftings or achievements. If our hearing were perfect, we would quickly become unbearably complacent. Others would undoubtedly start looking to us to provide instant oracles, instead of seeking the Lord for themselves.

We must humble ourselves, therefore, admit our mistakes, and, if at all possible, do our best to put matters right. It is the *enemy* who wants us to remain crushed by the memory of the times when we have got things wrong, and it is *perfectionists* who refuse to allow themselves (or others) to make any mistakes.

Perfectionism is a faulty model because it makes us strive to be or to achieve something that God never intended for us. To have high standards is entirely praiseworthy, but perfectionism is doomed to futility – the devil keeps advancing the 'finishing tape' a few meters ahead of our efforts to reach it.

Trying to live up to such misguided conceptions is like saying we want to run a four-minute mile in four kilograms! It means we are using all the wrong measuring rods. We risk being forever at the mercy of endless compulsiveness until we recognize it as an enemy tactic, and the very opposite of grace.

May the Lord help us to see how and why such obsessiveness developed in our lives. May we not 'worship in graveyards,' by looking to find inappropriate fulfillment from the wrong people and things. May He recalibrate our spirits away from the dictates of perfectionism to be more open to the leadings of His Spirit.

For Reflection and Prayer

> If I cherish iniquity in my heart, the Lord will not listen to me . . . Confess your sins to each other and pray for each other so that you may be healed. The prayer of a righteous man is powerful and effective. (Psalm 66:18, James 5:16)

If we find that we cannot rise above these tendencies and strongholds, we almost certainly need the help of someone who is less emotionally involved than we are. To quote my paraphrase of a well known advertisement: 'The prayers of others can reach the parts our own can not!' The question is, will you let them close enough to help?

When God fulfills His promise by another route

> Their faces had a new expression . . . All the sharpness and cunning and quarrelsomeness . . . seemed to have been washed away, and the courage and kindness which he had always had were easier to see. Perhaps it was talking with Aslan that had done it.[19]

Post-modernist orthodoxy would insist that chance and our own resourcefulness determine our destinies. May no hint of such attitudes stain our thinking! There is nothing random about the way God leads us. Meaning and purpose undergird every part of His dealings with us.

Shortly after I became a Christian, I made the conscious decision to do my best to consult the Lord before plunging in and doing my own thing. There have been times when I have got things upside down, and ended up way off the mark. On other occasions, God has honored the fact that I was trying to listen, and has made sure that I heard clearly when I needed to.

Returning to the 'leak of disappointment' that we looked at on pages eighty four to eighty six, we have seen quite a number of people over the years apply unsuccessfully for the ordained ministry. Because each one felt convinced that they had received a call from the Lord – and had done their best to test it – they often experience extreme confusion in the aftermath. They do not want to blame God, but the turmoil has to go somewhere. Round and round the questions pound. Had they been mistaken all along? Did the powers-that-be make the wrong decision in turning them down? Or were they simply not up to the required standard?

The pain is too intense to allow for any glib answers. If there has been presumption, may it be skimmed away – but where the call is genuine, God can still fulfill what He has promised, even if He does so by an entirely different route from the one we originally envisaged.

When Israel escaped from Egypt, the Lord did not lead them along the Inter-State to the Promised Land because that would have taken them through Philistine country. He knew that they were not yet ready to face a full-scale war, and that they would be tempted to flee back to Egypt at the first sign of conflict. He led them by the longer desert road, toward the Red Sea.[20]

The Lord likewise allows us many 'detours' – though when we are heading from A to B via C, D, E (and even Z as it sometimes feels!) it takes faith to believe that we will ever reach our destination. To the Lord, however, the journey is as important as the outcome.

On a walk beside a loch, Ros and I tried to take a track up a hill, but found it too muddy for our footwear. Rounding the corner, we spied a drier route. When we reached the summit, the Lord pointed out that although we had not been able to arrive at our destination in one go, we still reached it, albeit by a different route. Better still, we met Him there!

The walk serves as a parable of the way He so often leads us. We go all out for some initiative we feel the Lord is leading us to; we may even go public on it, only to find it fizzling out. We are left with 'egg on our faces,' but discover some time later (and mercifully it usually is sooner rather than later!) what it was that God really did have in mind for us.

These are the times when the snippet of Paul's teaching that we quoted on page ninety two really come alive: 'What you sow does not comes to life until it dies.' We, like the seed, *must* die to our own hopes before the Lord can cause them to multiply exponentially. Jesus implies the same in John 12:24.

The Lord knows exactly where He is taking us – and He wants all the glory to go to Him. This is why He allows us these dummy runs. We find these painful and confusing confusing, not least because they often *feel* like the real thing at the time. Beyond the present valley lie higher mountain tops for those with the courage and the vision to persevere.

For Reflection and Prayer

There is hope for a tree. If it is cut down, it will sprout again, and its new shoots will not fail. Its roots may grow old in the ground, and its stump die in the soil, yet at the scent of water it will bud and put forth shoots like a plant.

(Job 14:7-9)

Can you see how seeds that have fallen into the ground have surfaced again in your life? When God has fulfilled His promises in your life despite the setbacks on the way?

You are so much greater than our failures, Lord.
Even out of the soil of our failure
You weave new beginnings ,
and find fresh ways to accomplish Your purposes.
Ordain strength
from the depths of our brokenness,
so that we may grow in discernment
and bear more fruit in years to come,
In Jesus' name, Amen.

References

1 Henri Nouwen *The Genesee Diary* (Darton Longman & Todd Ltd) p.108

2 This is something we shall be exploring in much more detail in the sequel, *Led by the Spirit.*

3 Adrian Davies *The Quakers in English Society* 1655-1725 (Oxford) p.6

4 John 16:33

5 As it turned out, Anna did not look after Dominic when she moved to Shetland a few months later. Nevertheless, God used her call to Shetland as the first of many signs to confirm our own.

6 You can share in the incredible beauty of Shetland by visiting our web site www.ruachministries.org and visiting *Photo Galleries: The Shetland Collection, Surtout la Lumière* and *Shetland in Winter.*

7 Proverbs 24:6

8 Acts 20:22-23; 21:4. A helpful maxim to remember to help us discern the Lord's voice amidst the clamor that assail us: 'The Shepherd *leads*, but the butcher *drives.*'

9 C. S. Lewis *The Voyage of the Dawn Treader* (Harper Collins) pp. 178-9

10 Matthew 2:19-23. The Lord had previously warned the wise men in a dream not to return to King Herod. (Matthew 2:12)

11 Bob Mumford *Take Another Look at Guidance* (Lifechangers). I mention this important principle with some diffidence, because we have known occasions when an 'isolated' call has been enough to set us moving in important directions.

12 Paul Tillich *Systematic Theology* (University of Chicago Press) and *The Courage to be* (Yale University Press)

13 Acts 16:8-10 I can think of people who have passed over 'golden' opportunities in order to honor a prior call that God has placed on their lives. God does call us to 'give up' things as well as to receive – but He always finds ways to give back to us when we do so.

14 All too commonly, these tendencies manifest as 'Jezebel' spirits. See John Paul Jackson's important book *Unmasking the Jezebel Spirit* (Kingsway).

15 This three-layered net forms a pocket that traps the fish as they attempt to swim out.

16 Gordon MacDonald *Restoring Your Spiritual Passion* (Highland).

17 C. S. Lewis *The Horse and His Boy* (Harper Collins) pp. 164-5

18 C. S . Lewis *The Magician's Nephew* (Harper Collins) p. 197

19 C. S . Lewis *The Magician's Nephew* (Harper Collins) p. 197

20 Exodus 13:17.

Chapter Seven

Perspectives through Pressure

Peter and his companions were heavy with sleep, but when they were fully awake, they saw His glory, and two men standing with Him. Moses and Elijah, appeared in glorious splendor, talking with Jesus. They spoke about His suffering and departure, which He was about to bring to fulfillment at Jerusalem . . . While He was speaking, a cloud appeared and enveloped them – and they were afraid as they entered the cloud. (Luke 9:31,34)

When strong winds assail us from every angle, and troubles multiply, common sense may or may not incline us to do the right thing. In our own experience, we know how hard it is to cope with unrelenting pressure. Since *millions* of believers today are experiencing serious persecution for their faith, it is all the more important to pray that fear and tension do not crush our ability to discern the Still Small Voice when it really matters.

Before we look at some of the external pressures that come our way, there is one other type of face-to-face encounter which I did not mention earlier, and that is when the Lord Himself confronts us. Like Jacob, we will find that God sometimes contrives circumstances in such a way that we *have* to face up to His challenge.[1]

Face to face challenges

Brace yourself like a man; I will question you, and you shall answer Me . . . Have you journeyed to the springs of the sea, or walked in the recesses of the deep? (Job 38:3,16)

God uses people with broken and contrite spirits – those whose hearts have been made stronger (as opposed to harder) by the things that they have suffered. The enemy would much prefer that we were simply broken! There are few things he relishes more than goading believers into doing (or believing) things that God cannot own.

We saw at the end of the last chapter that the way we respond is all-important when the Lord sends His challenge. Those who humble themselves and repent, God will raise up, even if certain opportunities and platforms are no longer open to them. Those who do not are in real danger.

Countless promising ministries have fallen by the wayside because they drove through the red lights the Lord sent to warn them. To a greater or lesser extent they made the mistake of assuming that the Word of the Lord did not apply to them.

When the watcher angels delivered their dreadful verdict, one further year of grace was extended to the megalomaniac King Nebuchadnezzar before the hammer blow fell, and he was driven from his palace to live in abject humiliation. God did not restore him until seven long years had passed – and he had learned utterly necessary lessons of humility.[2]

Anyone who thinks that intimacy with God precludes such extreme measures should reread Hebrews 12. Jesus has very clear warnings to give believers on the subject of judgment. David Pawson suggests that all but two of the references to hell in the Gospel of Matthew are directed at born-again believers. It is a stunning warning against complacency and backsliding.[3]

Back in 1985, we went astray as a ministry team over a particular issue. One day the Lord spoke clearly that although I was going to find it hard to hear, He was going to close the ministry down. This came as an enormous shock to us, as it usually does when the Lord intervenes so drastically.

Beyond the initial grief lay much heart searching – but also much mercy. Having dismantled the previous team, the Lord moved swiftly to bring together a far more experienced team, who were able to achieve much more than the previous one would have been capable of doing.

For Reflection and Prayer

If you feel as though you are going through a refining, or even a dismantling process, it is best to face it squarely, and even to welcome it. Take heart from the example of Hezekiah. Unlike many kings in their latter years, he did not waste time arguing with the Lord's verdict, but emerged from a life-threatening situation full of determination to walk humbly before the Lord all the days of his life. We can make his prayer ours.

> *I will walk humbly all my years*
> *because of this anguish of my soul.*
> *Lord by such things men live;*
> *and my spirit finds life in them.*
> *You restored me to health and let me live.*
> *Surely it was for my benefit*
> *that I suffered such anguish.*
> *In Your love You kept me from the pit of destruction;*
> *You have put all my sins behind Your back.*
> *(Isaiah 38:16-17)*

When the fog horn sounds, guess what lies ahead?

This man is My chosen instrument to carry My name before the Gentiles and their kings and before the people of Israel. I will show him how much he must suffer for My name. (Acts 9:16)

Right from the outset of his ministry, the Lord told Paul plainly, what he would suffer for the sake of the Kingdom.[4]

Just before we moved to Shetland, the Lord warned me that someone there was going to dig her knife deep in Ros's back. Having steered the maternity services in another region through an emotionally demanding period, this was the last thing we wanted to hear.

It did not take long for what the Lord had predicted to materialize. Ros enjoyed an outstanding relationship with the

Shetlandic women she cared for, but someone who was in a position to cause her immense difficulty set out to do everything she could to oppose her. Like Alexander the Coppersmith, who did so much harm to Paul, this person's constant attacks took a huge toll on us, both physically and emotionally.

Although the pain caused by this person's threats and misrepresentations was excruciating, at least we never wasted time wondering if we had strayed out of God's will in coming to Shetland. The Lord had been so wise in giving us such a clear-cut call.

Quite simply, *Fire from the North* (the international prayer conference we organized that brought representatives together from across the northern nations) would never have come about had we not persevered through what often felt like unbearable pressure.

Apart from Ros's situation at work, we were under no illusions concerning the difficulties this call posed. For a start, I had no contact with Scandinavian Christians. My concern was that even if they did get to hear about it, might they not find the costs of getting to Shetland too great? It hardly seemed an ideal location for an international conference. Moreover, Christians on Shetland had never hosted a conference for people from off the island, and a number of key people were decidedly unenthusiastic . . . would they rise to the occasion? I proceeded with the all-important practical preparations, but inwardly I needed additional reassurance to use as a shield against the 'but what ifferies' that hammered away in my head in the middle of the night.

It was on a ferry crossing that the Lord penetrated my cloud and spoke four profoundly reassuring things:

i) 'You will be surprised by who I bring to Shetland.

(I was.)

ii) 'My deep peace will come.' (It certainly did.)

iii) 'I will cover the costs of the Conference week.' (He did.)

iv) 'When Moses was struggling to lead the Israelite people
through the wilderness, he prayed, "Unless You come up
with us, Lord, what's the point of going on?" Notice that
he never said, "Lord, You're not going up with us, so I'm
not going one step further!" If Moses had taken that approach, you would have heard no more about him. It was
that word 'unless' that kept the door open just wide enough
to give Me the chance to come through for him. I want you
to do the same.'

For Reflection and Prayer

*Thank You Lord that Moses trusted You –
and You strode to his rescue.
Be with all who feel like giving up today.
Send Your angels to ease the pressure
and Your Holy Spirit to bring conviction of sin,
especially on . . . and . . .
Help them to use the warfare verses of Scripture
as a shield against confusion and despair,
and as weapons of faith to advance Your Kingdom.
In Jesus' name, Amen.*

Light before entering the tunnel

You are going to have the light just a little while longer.
Walk while you have the light, before darkness overtakes
you . . . Do not be afraid of what you are about to suffer. I
tell you, the devil will put some of you in prison to test you,
and you will suffer persecution for ten days. Be faithful
unto death.   (John 12:35; Revelation 2:10.)

Following the will of the Lord sometimes leads us into the
zone of maximum conflict – just as it did for Jesus Himself.
The more significant the project, the more intense the attacks
are likely to be.

The Lord sometimes draws especially close just before
trouble comes our way. It is important not to be neurotic
about this: the Lord doesn't *only* come near when there is
rough weather ahead. Neither should we blame Him when the
difficult times arrive. The trials were already on their way: it

was simply His kindness to alert us in advance, and to give us some specific word or a special sense of His presence to hang on to.

It was while Ros and I were enjoying a few days holiday in Pembrokeshire that the Lord dropped His bombshell. He told me that we were about to go through such an intensely difficult time that we would only be able to cope by remembering how He had delivered us in the past from seemingly impossible situations. (We certainly do have many testimonies of how the Lord has 'airlifted' us out of difficult dilemmas, but when the pressure is really on, it is easy to feel overwhelmed, and to forget to use the memory of these deliverances as a 'springboard' for faith.)

Almost immediately, the attacks against Ros intensified. We were plunged into an unremittingly grim ordeal. A friend had a picture that the doors of our house were being so tightly guarded that Ros had no option but to climb into a basket outside the bedroom wall and make good her escape.

Others 'saw' this basket attached to the hot-air balloon that we mentioned previously that whisked us off the island. Like Saul, who had to be placed in a basket and let down the city wall of Damascus, Ros's departure from Shetland was both swift and traumatic. By the Lord's mercy, however, it enabled us to reach the next stage of our pilgrimage.

For Reflection and Prayer

When God is going to do something important, He allows us to see the difficulties first. When He is going to do something magnificent, however, He allows it to appear completely impossible.

'Customise' this challenging thought to specific situations that you are currently concerned about.

When the pressure piles on . . .

I know that through your prayers and the help given by the Spirit of Jesus Christ, what has happened to me will turn out for my deliverance. (Philippians 1:19)

In various places, Paul lists the persecutions he went through: horrendous experiences that Luke, for the most part, does not even see fit to mention in the Acts of the Apostles. They are a graphic illustration of the intense storms that the devil rouses against God's key apostles.

On three occasions Paul was beaten with rods. Contemporary descriptions reveal this to have been a horrifying ordeal. He was also shipwrecked three times, spending a whole night and a day adrift in the ocean on one occasion. A lesser man could easily have decided that 'enough is enough,' and refrained from setting out on any more perilous journeys.

I remember hearing Billy Graham speaking in Oxford the day after he had just fallen in the shower and broken some ribs. He confessed that, like any other sixty-year old, he would dearly like to put his feet up and play golf. Because he knew the unique calling that God had placed on his life, however, he kept going for a further twenty years of remarkable front line service.

One evening, during a series of meetings in the Town Hall, anarchists burst in, letting off fire alarms, cutting TV cables and shouting obscenities. The sense of evil was palpable – yet more people responded to his gospel message that evening than any other. It is a great mistake to suppose that the Lord is not working simply because storms are raging. Even when evil does strike, the Lord can still bring good out of it.

The Chinese word for crisis is made up of two characters. One, predictably, translates as 'danger.' The other contains a more intriguing connotation: that of 'opportunity.' Within every crisis lies the possibility that God will intervene to turn things round, and accomplish something entirely new.

Remember the angels who strengthened Elijah, Daniel, Jesus and Paul in their times of greatest need! Scripture shows clearly what a vital role God's heavenly messengers have to play in helping us accomplish the Lord's assignments.

Given that most of us are not experiencing physical persecution, it is easy to feel that our plight barely registers on the

Richter scale of suffering – especially when set alongside what so many of our brothers and sisters are going through in other parts of the world. The Lord does not underestimate the pain involved in being judged, controlled and misconstrued, however.

Worse still, we have felt the twisting knife thrusts of accusing thoughts, deep within our soul. Condemnation is such a powerful foe because it is tailor-made to exploit our particular weaknesses. In the privacy of our hearts, we are tempted to play and replay the words and events that have caused us so much anguish – and the enemy's verdict on them.

Left unchecked, these far from still small voices can crush our faith to the point where we are willing to tone down the scale of our Christian service. It is as though the powers of darkness dangle an unwritten contract before our eyes: 'If you will just stop troubling me, I will leave you alone!'

All this takes places at a subliminal level, of course. Mercifully, more often than not, the devil overplays his hand and we realize what is going on.

Refuse the compromise. Don't give in. Come out of your corner, with weapons of faith blazing! Above all, do not allow your spirit to become 'stuck' because of things that people have said or done. 'Anything is possible,' Charles Finney reminds us, 'provided only that we are willing to forgive.' In the name of Jesus, forgive the parents, siblings, offspring, colleagues, employers, pastors, and whoever else it may be who has caused you such distress.

For Reflection and Prayer

Lord, in Your name we bless and forgive
those who have proved over-protective,
under-imaginative,
or downright wrong in their counsel.
We also ask Your forgiveness for all the times
when we have been unable to discern
what You were doing in someone else's life,
and have disturbed their peace as a result.
In Jesus' name, Amen.

Seek God and Hold Firm!

> If anyone is to go into captivity, into captivity they will go
> . . . This calls for patient endurance and faithfulness on the
> part of the saints. (Revelation 13:10)

A friend of ours used to minister behind the Iron Curtain. One afternoon he made his way to a barn in the country. It being considered too dangerous to announce details of the meeting openly, the believers had to seek the Lord as to when and where it would be held. My friend was amazed to find the barn full to overflowing. When he asked what they would like him to speak on, he was even more humbled when they replied, 'Teach us more about listening, please; we are not very good at it.' You could have fooled him!

We are wise if we make it our goal to seek the Lord with just as much determination as these Russian believers, even without the stimulus of overt persecution. There is nothing in Scripture to indicate that God intended such intimacy to be reserved exclusively for times of crisis.

When we are going through times of intense pressure, most of us are desperate to hear the Lord telling us what He is going to do to rescue us from our trials. It is worth reflecting, and for more than a moment, on the greater things the Lord often achieves by *not* leaping to answer our 'Get-me-out-of-here, I'm a Christian' type of prayers.

John Bunyan, the seventeenth century non Conformist preacher and writer, chose to remain in prison rather than bow to the authority's proposal to release him immediately – provided he agreed to hold no more public meetings.

Tormented by the love he felt for his family (especially his blind young daughter) Bunyan found the hardest thing to bear were the pleas of so-called friends. They not only urged him to accept these poison-tipped offers, but even dared to tell him that the stand he was taking amounted to nothing less than a dereliction of his duty towards his family!

Under the influence of what he later came to characterize as Giant Despair, John Bunyan wrote, 'I felt as though I was pulling the roof down over my own head, but I must do it, I must.' It was while he was in prison that he wrote *Pilgrim's Progress* – quite possibly the most influential Christian book of all time.

Think, too, of all the inmates who came to faith in Ravensbruck concentration camp precisely because the Lord did *not* protect Corrie Ten Boon and her family from being betrayed. When He subsequently arranged for her release (through a clerical error!) she was the only member of her family to survive. Far from succumbing to an old age full of perpetual grief and bitterness, she set up a ministry to serve emotionally damaged victims of the war – exactly as her sister had foreseen in a dream.

Millions have subsequently read Corrie's books, or watched the film *The Hiding Place*. How grateful we can be that saints like these refused to compromise.

For Reflection and Prayer
For the joy that was set before You, Lord Jesus,
You went up to Jerusalem
fully aware of all You were going to suffer.
If You have more to do in us through the pressure
that we and so many of Your people are experiencing,
may we set our faces like flint
and keep on reaching out to You.
May we live each day to the full,
make good use of the opportunities You send our way,
and find fresh ways to serveYou.
In the name of the One who ushered in the Kingdom by
refusing to opt out, Amen.

Put a brick through the magnifying glass

I compare the troubles which we have to undergo in the course of the year to a great bundle of faggots, far too large for us to lift. But God does not require us to carry the whole at once. He mercifully unties the bundle, and gives us first one stick, which we are to carry today, and then another, which we are to carry tomorrow, and so on. This we might easily manage, if we would only take the burden appointed for each day; but we choose to increase our troubles by carrying yesterday's stick over again today, and adding tomorrow's burden to the load, before we are required to bear it. (John Newton).

Where does pressure build up most strongly? In our minds! Alex Buchanan once declared the enemy's favourite weapon to be a magnifying glass. When he shines his glass on an issue, we tend to focus so intensely on some scheme, situation or squabble that we find it hard to think of anything else.

The powers of darkness love to shine their high magnitude glass on suitably selected issues, and then watch us writhe. They go flat out to inject unhelpful thoughts *into* our mind, and to keep other considerations *out*. Because soul and spirit run so close together, they often succeed in focusing their glass on something that began as a genuine burden in the spirit, but then make determined attempts to twist it into something 'soulish.'

If the father of lies is involved in the situation, there is always the risk of being deceived. Twenty-seven years ago, on a long coach journey, a haze of well-being settled on me: a warm fuzzy environment that was entirely conducive for the reception of weird and wonderful imaginings.

This was when I 'heard' that I was going to marry someone whose passion for the Lord had bowled me over. There was no substance whatsoever to these thoughts, but they were intense enough to get me excited at the time, until a reality check punctured the balloon and brought my hopes to naught.

Such experiences remind us how close the deceiver lurks, and how easily our emotions can be led astray. That is why we cannot stress too strongly how wary we should be of considering any one 'word' on its own to constitute genuine guidance, unless it is confirmed in other ways.

Because the Lord gives grace as and when we need it, the powers of darkness much prefer us to be taken up with *imaginary* fears and problems, for which no real grace can be available. Saints, we don't need to fall for this sucker punch, or to stand for this torture. The power of God is so much greater than our problems *or* our failings!

For Reflection and Prayer

Keep us, Lord, from filling our minds with fantasies —
for if the act is wrong, then so too is the intention.
Lord, we confess wrong thoughts and deeds to You
before we rationalize them
and deny that they are wrong.
In Jesus' name we give you now the matter of . . .

Put a brick through whatever magnifying glass
is being shone into our minds!
Disentangle emotions and delusions
that are choking the flow of Your Spirit in our spirit.
In Jesus' name, Amen.

Scrambling the scrambler

For every situation that we face, God has a promise to match it in His Word. The more we use these promises, the greater the threat we pose the powers of darkness. No wonder they do all they can to make it difficult for us to understand what God is saying. Distractions, distortions, accusations, self-doubts: the father of lies goes to great lengths to misrepresent the nature of God to us – and to get God's people slandering each other behind their back.

Some years ago I visited a village where the church was being torn apart by spirits of division. I asked the Lord how to address the issue without sounding patronizing. His answer took me by surprise. 'Play a game of Chinese whispers!'

I divided the group into a large circle, and whispered a silly message to the person next to me, and then waited with interest to see what shape it would emerge in at the other end. 'Six hundred sausages in a cemetery' ended up as 'I shot myself last Saturday!' One by one, people realized how scrambled their lines of communication had become.

Without building a theology around them, several of Frank Peretti's novels (*This Present Darkness* and *Piercing the Darkness*)[5] contain powerful pointers to the way the powers of darkness pepper our minds with distractions on the one hand, and gales of accusations on the other. Peretti's books also remind us how important it is to respond when the Holy Spirit prompts us to pray. May the Lord's people be alert to overcome all the devil's efforts to scramble our lines of communication!

For Reflection and Prayer

When the most unexpected people oppose, resist and reject us, it may be a sign that we are in exactly the *right* place. The fact that there is such intense warfare indicates that the kingdom of darkness is seriously worried.

What are the ways by which he is trying to stop you from attempting all the Lord has put within your heart? Don't let him succeed!

Praise that pierces the darkness

Nothing predisposes us to discern the Still Small Voice better than a spirit of praise and worship. The very praise that is so precious to the Lord is an acrid stench in Satan's nostrils. He loathes it!

Judson Cornwall tells a magnificent story in *Let Us Praise* about the way worship scatters the powers of darkness.[6] After months of demonic forces oppressing services in his church, Judson felt obliged to bring the service to a full stop in order to bind the powers of darkness.

One day the Lord revealed something that came as a shock: that the demons, in their perverted way, regarded it as a great success that the believers should focus on them – so much so that they were coming from far and wide to disrupt the services. God told Judson how dishonoring this was to Him, and that if they would concentrate on worshipping Him, He would take care of the demonic presence.

When the heaviness reappeared the following week, every-one looked at expectantly to their pastor. But Judson had taken the message to heart, and continued to worship God. True to His word, the Lord stretched out His hand and sent the heaviness packing.

Howls of horror are heard in the demonic kingdom when the people of God rise up in worship and prayer. The power of God is released, and the devils are forced to flee – often turning against themselves in the process.

For Reflection and Prayer
Lord, You are the One
who brings us through each storm.
You are the stillness after the turmoil,
and our peace at the end of the day.
Keep us in the spirit of thanksgiving,
for this will glorify You,
and counteract our tendency to moan.

References

[1] Genesis 32:24

[2] Daniel 4:17-37

[3] David Pawson, *Unlocking the Bible* (Collins) pp. 825-6

[4] E.g. 2 Corinithians 11:25-28. Truth, as we know, is always the best psychology. Knowing how easily we are deterred, however, the Lord sometimes chooses to say nothing for the time being about certain trials that lie ahead for us!

[5] Frank Peretti's novels are published by Crossway Books.

[6] Hundreds of thousands of people have found the writings of Merlin Carruthers pivotal in developing an understanding of the power and Biblical rationale behind praising God at all times.

Chapter Eight

Strategic Listening

Serve only the Lord your God and fear Him alone. *Obey* his commands, *listen* to His voice, and *cling* to Him.

(Deuteronomy 13:4)

From the vantage point of Mount Hermon, the Lord Jesus looked down over both Israel and Syria, and, in spirit, out over the whole world. He knew that His disciples were shortly to embark on the greatest mission of transformation the world has ever seen. He knew that they would come face to face with many extreme needs, and encounter such intense opposition, that they would need to listen carefully to the Still Small Voice.

If strategy is the key to success in business and military circles, why should it be any less so in the realm of listening to the Lord? The Still Small Voice reveals a portion of the Commander's plan, so that we can play our full part in the work of the Kingdom. If we do not learn to think strategically, then, like a ship that never ventures far from shore, our listening is likely to remain focused on matters close to home and heart.

Harnessing the power of God

God has committed some work to me, which He has not committed to another. I have my mission. (John Newman)

Every time we meet with other Christians, whether on the phone or face to face, we discuss people and issues that are 'prayer-worthy.' So much the better if we go the extra mile, and commit matters to the Lord in prayer – preferably there and then.[1] Just as countries rich in water harness its immense force to make hydro-electricity, so we must 'tap into' the power of God through prayer.

It is when we turn from information-sharing and reflect back to the Lord the news, the needs and the nations that He has been laying on our hearts, meetings become encounters. The key is to say 'Let's pray together,' and to *give* God the opportunity to move in power.

Derek Prince relates how the Lord told him to warn the Kenyan Christians not to make the same mistake Pentecostals have so often made, squandering His presence and His power in spiritual self-indulgence. As he called the conference to pray for their nation,[2] a man had a vision of a great evil advancing towards their country. It was turned away at the last minute as the result of their prayers.

It is good to experiment with different ways of doing this. At times it may be most appropriate to adopt the model widely used in South Korea, with everyone raising their voice and crying out to the Lord at the same time, very much as the apostles must have done in Acts 4. At other times we will benefit more by developing the Quaker emphasis of waiting quietly for the Spirit to lead and direct us.[3]

May the Lord help us to remember people and places we usually contrive to forget.[4] Brother Andrew was leading a prayer meeting once in his home town, for prisoners behind the Iron Curtain. In the middle of it, news was brought to them that a girl who everyone present knew was seriously ill. The level of intensity shot up as people poured out their hearts in prayer.

The Lord restored the young lady, but did so in such a way that expanded everyone's confidence that their prayers really were touching God's throne.

'You are concerned about this girl because you know her,' the Lord said, 'but I am equally as concerned for the people you are praying about in these other countries, whom you have never met.'

If we can dare to 'analyze' what it was that made this time of prayer so special, I would suggest two key characteristics.

Firstly, God honored the fact that people were prepared to to look beyond themselves, and identify with people who are deeply scored on God's heart.

Secondly, the friendship between the members of the group made it easy for Him to answer prayer. We usually pray and listen best when we *trust* the people we are with, and when we are not thinking about whether we are sounding too judgmental or political – or getting our grammar wrong!

For Reflection and Prayer

Gordon MacDonald claims that one draft horse can pull two tons of weight, but that two can pull more than twenty! Take this extraordinary example of exponential increase to heart. I liken it to Jesus' teaching that where two or three come together in agreement, He is right there in our midst. What an encouragement to find ways to harness our friendships for the Lord in prayer, as well as in other forms of service.

Father, right now we agree that
as Your Still Small Voice prompts,
we will overcome our fear and reluctance
and say 'Let's pray together.'

Authority in prayer

The Transfiguration shows us that the ultimate seat of authority resides in the courts of Heaven. But Scripture also reminds us to pray for the seats of power around the world, imperfect though they are.

You may, or may not, have experienced the sort of authority Suzanne Pillans displayed when she prayed for the sick in Africa. (That opening chapter feels a long way away now, doesn't it!) It is no coincidence that so many of the prayers in the New Testament take the form of commands.

Early in Jesus' ministry,[5] He promised the disciples that they would see 'still greater things.' When He stilled the storm with a word of command, and raised Lazarus from the dead, we see these words coming true.

In John 14:12, Jesus looks forward to the day when His disciples would exercise the same authority. Heeding the Still Small Voice, and moving in real faith, they would cast out spirits of divination, restore the dead to life and heal the sick – just as Jesus Himself had done.[6]

The powers of darkness understand the power of prayer much better than most Christians do. After all, they have had centuries of being defeated by praying saints. That is why they do all they can to prevent us using the authority that is rightly ours in Christ Jesus.

Many years ago, at a meeting in the Cotswolds, I felt the Lord warning me that the IRA were planning to detonate a bomb. As everyone cried out to God together, the Lord gave me one prayer above the hubbub: 'Lord, defuse bombs to-night!' Some hours later an IRA bomb was discovered in London and defused safely.

When the Spirit stirs within us, it is vitally important that we do not dismiss it as coincidence. The Lord uses the prayers of His servants in such ways to *lessen* – though not necessarily to avert entirely – many judgments and disasters. Two weeks before the Twin Towers were destroyed, the Lord told David Wilkerson to stop all activities in his church in Times Square, New York, and to focus exclusively on prayer. We will never know how many *more* people might have lost their lives had the congregation not interceded.

More recently, following the terrorist bombs in London on 7/7/05, Ros felt a nudge to pray that other bombs would be found intact. It sounded a tall order, but four deadly devices were safely dismantled just two weeks later in the London Underground and on a bus. The government declared we were extremely "lucky!"

As we have been hinting, the Lord wants us to be as concerned for nations as we are for individuals, and to be equally at home in praying for either. What impressed David

Watson most when he met Corrie Ten Boom was the natural way in which she turned to the Lord, lifting everything from missing car keys to international crises to Him.

Such authority works at every level. From time to time I experience in my own body some unusual symptom as I am praying with someone, in order to point me in the direction where they are hurting. I was praying on the phone the other day for someone who had been plagued by a sore throat for several months. Suddenly, it felt as though I had a kilo of sand in my own throat. Such sensations have a wonderful ways of making us pray full-on. It lifted as I prayed, and my friend's throat was completely healed as well.

There are times when simply committing something to the Lord does not appear to be enough. We need to exercise the spiritual authority the Lord has given us.

A few months ago, I injured my back lifting a box that was too heavy for me. I was in extreme pain, so much so that it was taking me five minutes to lower myself into bed, and considerably longer to get out again. We were due to go away for the weekend, but there was no way that I was going anywhere unless the Lord did a miracle.

If ever there was a time to exercise authority in prayer this was it. Ros took that authority, and, within minutes, eighty per cent of the pain had disappeared. The Lord developed such important relationships that weekend that I shudder to think of all that would have been missed had she not done so.

For Reflection and Prayer

As we considered on page one hundred and sixteen and seventeen, there is a fine line between exercising genuine spiritual authority, and straying wide of the mark into presumption. We will by no means always get the balance right – but neither should we allow our fear of overstepping the mark to hold us back from praying with the authority the Lord gives.

Lord, may Your Still Small Voice lead and direct our prayers. Keep us from presumption, and release Your

authentic power into many situations – starting with the
ones I bring to You right now . . .

Bearing burdens in the Spirit

The world scoffs at the thought of a man weeping for his
neighbor's sins as if for his own, or even more than for his
own, for it seems contrary to nature. But the love which
brings it about is not of this world. (Angela of Foligno)

The Still Small Voice can 'activate' anything we hear, read or
see, and call us to pray about it. This, in essence, is burden-
bearing. It is a high calling because it originates with the Holy
Spirit prompting us to intercede (as opposed to us going to
God with our own concerns). As Angela points out in our
starting quote, we require both generosity of spirit and
unwavering love to persist in it.

As we cultivate the silence we spoke of earlier, people's
needs stand before us with a sharpness and a vividness that
rarely happens if we are too caught up in busyness.

The more sensitive we are, the more likely we are to pick
up the hurts and tensions that people are carrying – even the
ones that they themselves are unaware of. This puts a double
burden on us: the prayer burden itself, plus the fact that the
person is blind to it. Because it is not always possible to bring
the matter safely into the open, we must continue to bear the
burden in prayer.

On page one hundred and thirty four, we considered how
something that starts out as a genuine burden can end up
weighing us down. If the 'burden' does not flow through us
to the Cross, these needs and tensions risk becoming attached
to our soul – much as sticks in a stream can snag in bushes
on their course downstream. Soul ties and psychological
transference easily develop at this stage, greatly confusing
and sometimes all but nullifying the burden-bearing process.
Certain emotions may feel profoundly 'spiritual' at the time,
but prove later to have been based on something entirely
different. This is certainly something to be aware of.

Another tendency some of us are prone to is to internalize the tensions our spirit is picking up, and assume that *we* must be in some way responsible for it. Although in some cases there may be some truth in this, more often than not the tension was pre-existing, and entirely independent of us.

If we do not realize this, we can paralyze ourselves with condemnation and concern, instead of releasing faith into the situation.

Shortly after we were married, Rosalind and I experienced an occasion when we became extremely tense and irritated with each other. It crossed my mind that the Lord might be using our experience to highlight the intense spiritual warfare that is being directed against Christian marriages.

I heard later that at the exact moment of our explosion, a man in our congregation had burst out in violence, and told his wife that he was leaving her. Mercifully he thought better of it. I wish I could say that we *only* get uptight with each other when we are identifying with other people's problems!

To take another rather extreme example, I remember Ros starting to manifest symptoms similar to those of a woman we had just visited in a psychiatric hospital. We had forgotten to set ourselves prayerfully free after the visit. It took a several minutes of intensive spiritual warfare style prayers before Ros felt released.

On other occasions when we have been involved in spiritual warfare and have forgotten to 'cut ourselves off,' we have experienced disturbing dreams. It is right to be alert, but not fearful. God gives us the ability to take authority over all such things.

What we must never do is to assume that we can 'magic' problems away from people who are not prepared to seek the Lord for themselves. 'Burden bearing' can lift off a percentage of people's problems, but only to the point where they are sufficiently detached from whatever it is that has been weighing them down that they can choose for themselves how they will respond.

The more we are prepared to identify with the people we are praying for, the more fruit we will bear – so long as we do not allow our concern to lead us into making 'substitutionary' prayers.

In plainer English, this means not praying something like, 'Let me take this person's illness so that they can go free.' Since Jesus died to set us free, it would be quite wrong to interpose ourselves as mediators.

Neither should we underestimate the toll burden-bearing takes on us. It is serious work, and it is important that we take time away from the 'soul' face. The very same sensitivity that enables us to pick up on people's hurts and needs becomes a liability if we start to feel *overly* responsible for their welfare.

This is where something that looks like godly persistence can lead us to persevere in situations we would do much better to walk away from.

Given the sheer amount of information that comes our way, however, we may *need* to set up some mental and practical boundaries and barriers. Information-overload, along with compassion fatigue, are all part of the devil's attempts to exhaust us with burdens we were never meant to take up.

Establishing this balance has another positive benefit. It prevents us from deriving too great a percentage of our self-worth from what the Lord does through us on behalf of others.

God loves us for who we are – not only for the times when His Spirit soars and sighs through us in mountain-moving intercession.

Joyful attitudes are a brilliant witness, and do much for our inner well-being. Genuine fun and simple pleasures are likewise powerful weapons against the enemy. Even a smile can make such a difference.

As the Lord once reminded me, 'When I made children with an instinct for play, I was putting something of My own nature in them. You are out of balance, My children, if you do not play!'

For Reflection and Prayer

'Who is weak and I do not feel weak?' asked Paul. 'Who is
led into sin and I do not inwardly burn?' (2 Corinthians
11:29, cf Romans 8:26-27)

The Lord calls us to pray for some people, professions,
communities and nations on a regular basis, but to lift others
to Him as and when they come to mind. Who or what has He
most strongly placed on your heart?

Lord, grant me the ability to carry burdens for You.
Free me from any hurts or guilts
that would hinder me from being able to do so safely.
Reposition any burdens that have strayed into my soul,
and help me to carry them in the Spirit
until they are prayed though to completion,
or the time comes when You release me from them.
In Jesus' name, Amen.

Prayers of mourning and identification

'But please, please, won't you – can't you give me something that will cure mother?' Up till then [Digory] had been
looking at the Lion's great feet . . . now, in his despair, he
looked up at its face. What he saw surprised him as much
as anything in his whole life. The tawny face was bent
down near his own and great shining tears shone in the
lion's eyes . . . For a moment he felt as if the lion must
really be sorrier about his mother than he was himself![7]

Listening prepares us for our ultimate calling, which is to be
partners with the Lord in this world and the next. We do not
seek to hear the Still Small Voice out of curiosity, but rather
so that we may experience more of His compassion. God does
not *despair* over the state of the world; He *mourns* over it.
This is a profoundly spiritual response, as opposed to worldly
hand-wringing that accomplishes precisely nothing.[8]

Remember all the times the Lord Jesus was 'moved with
compassion?' The Greek word used here is a very strong one.
(It is the one used to describe movements of the bowels!)

When Jesus felt such intense emotion, just look at what happened. Remarkable miracles followed hard on the heels of Him responding to the crowds who had no food, to those who were without sight and afflicted, or to the widow at Nain whose son had died.[9]

When we feel particularly moved by the expression on someone's face – or the plight they find themselves in – pray in the Spirit for them. Even when we are traveling, or about our daily business, we may find intense longings – groans that words cannot express[10] stirring within us – as we see the emptiness in people's lives.

There are times when we must come to the Lord kneeling not standing, crying not laughing. 'Tears are the highest form of prayer,' the Jewish Rabbis declared. They touch and release our hardened emotions and can overcome all things.

There is no greater pain than that of love which is rejected, as the parents of any wayward child know only too well. The more secure we are in the love of God, the more we can respond to the grief the Lord feels over the state of the world. If Jesus does not despair, then neither must we. It is precisely because we have such a sure and certain hope that we can allow the Still Small Voice to lead us along pathways of mourning in spirit and burden-bearing in prayer.

I tried to share this concept with a lively worship leader the other day. 'Just as surely as high praise and affirmation are appropriate in one context,' I argued, 'so tears and mourning are in another.' I proceeded to show him a verse that means a lot to me: 'The heart of the wise is in the house of mourning.'[11] It provoked a surprisingly strong negative reaction in him. 'I'd like to see that verse torn out of the Bible!' he declared. To me, however, it encapsulates an awareness that should be embedded in the heart of all who seek to heed the Still Small Voice.

Our tears are like the bass notes that complement and complete the treble ones of our praise and worship. On its own, the treble clef might become shrill, making our worship self-indulgent. The bass clef on *its* own, might become melancholic, morbid even, without a spring of living praise flowing through our hearts. It is when the two are in balance that we reflect the Lord's heart best.

Do you remember how 'deeply moved and troubled in spirit' Jesus was when he heard about Lazarus' death?[12] The Greek word for 'troubled' is terasso – which means 'stirred up' or 'profoundly agitated.'

In the center of old fashioned twin tub washing machines lay an 'agitator,' that thrashed and beat the clothes clean. Many of us know only too much about being 'agitated' in such ways. The secret is to turn this inner turmoil into prayer, crying out to the Lord for Him to turn whatever it is that is troubling us into a blessing.

So long as it does not degenerate into soulish melancholia, such mourning can therefore be a true and important way to express the Lord's compassion. As members of the one family, God wants us to share in what our brothers and sisters are suffering in the Middle East, in Africa, China, North Korea and other countries where persecution is rife. We saw earlier how God honors this willingness to look wider than our own immediate circumstances. Scripture urges us to *'Remember those who are in prison as if you were fellow prisoners and those who are ill-treated as if you yourselves were suffering.'*[13]

When judgment fell in Ezekiel's day, the Lord sovereignly spared all who were grieved over the detestable sins of those around them.[14] Jeremiah so longed for his people to return to God that he cried out, 'Oh, that my head were a spring of water, my eyes a fountain of tears.'[15]

John Knox knelt and prayed in the snow, pleading for mercy for Scotland, and the Lord heard his heartfelt prayers and moved across the nation. When James Fraser went to minister amongst the Lisu tribe, he found the going so hard that he deliberately set out to round up the saints back home. He urged them to play as full a part in the spiritual battle as he himself was doing. Months of persistent persevering prayer led to the power of God breaking through – spectacularly![16]

Most traditional church activities contain little allusion to the realities of this spiritual warfare – yet every day millions are raped, abused, aborted or led astray. It is when we seek the Lord with *all* our heart that we find Him. Such urgency is essential if we are to advance beyond the superficial in our prayer and listening.

For Reflection and Prayer

I asked the Lord once to show me how I was doing as a burden-bearer. By way of a reply, He showed me a picture of an eastern lady carrying a pitcher on her head with no apparent effort. When I tried to the same, the pitcher slipped from my head to my shoulders, with the result that I was staggering along, bent almost double.

'Ok, Lord,' I said, 'what's the trick?'

'The secret of carrying burdens,' the Lord revealed (and he was not talking about pitchers of water) 'lies in poise, posture and practice.' May He develop more of these qualities in us.

Identificational Repentance

> Revivals must often start with an apology. God will not work strongly where His people are divided. Rapid spiritual growth will never come in a community with lingering resentment or bitterness . . . That's why we need Reconciliation. (James Rutz)[17]

Identificational Repentance (or I.R. as it is sometimes known) is increasingly being recognized as a powerful way to break certain types of spiritual blockages – perhaps, in some cases, the *only* way. At its simplest, it consists of asking forgiveness both of God and of other people (especially people groups) for sins that have been committed in the past.

This is no sentimental foolishness, or deluded attempt to parcel out our personal or national sense of shame. It is an entirely biblical way of tapping into the power of God to heal.

Nothing could better reflect the ways of the Kingdom, or take us further away from the self-serving spirit that characterizes empire-builders. In the process, strongholds that the enemy may have set in place generations ago are challenged, and in some cases removed.[18]

Countless people have been inspired to go further along the intercessory road as a result of reading the testimony of Rees Howells. God called this Welsh miner to a narrow pathway of prayerful identification on behalf of the suffering and afflicted. He and his team of intercessors at the Bible College of Wales waged a spiritual battle alongside the physical conflict throughout the Second World War.

The story of the radical prayers that God led Rees Howells to pray is all but essential reading for those who desire to let the Still Small Voice direct them into interceding for wider matters. I will refrain from sharing more of his testimony here. Suffice it to say that they had a major impact on the outcome of the War – and you will benefit more by obtaining a copy of the book for yourself.[19]

In all this, we are following in the footsteps of our Master. When the Spirit came strongly on the Lord Jesus in the Garden of Gethsemane, He responded with 'loud cries and tears.'[20] William Barclay says that the Greek expression used here, *krauge,* is a very strong one. It speaks of a cry which is wrung from someone him in the stress of some tremendous tension or searing pain – such as torture.

This is burden-bearing at its most intense – and these are the times when breakthroughs occur in the Heavenly places. When we read in Luke 22:44 that Jesus 'prayed more earnestly' the translation barely hints at what was really going on. The word literally means 'more stretched-outedly.' As the pressure intensified and bore down on Him, Jesus was at the very limit of His ability to endure.

At this crucial time, Jesus found Himself effectively as much on His own as He would be in a few hours time on the cross. It is only when we consider all that emerged from this intense agonizing in spirit that we begin to appreciate more fully the power of intercession.

In our quest to be *shaping* history rather than just participating in it, we will scale much greater heights if we are linked with people who have a similar heart and spirit. It is together that we can make a real difference.

For Reflection and Prayer

Lord, make our hearts as soft as Yours,
so that we can experience more of Your compassion,
and persevere in prayer
until the power of Heaven breaks through.

Heavenly music

The voices were many, for all in the tent seemed worshipping; the sound was one, the co-mingled sound of many waters. No drilled choir could have kept in such harmony and unity, with sweetest melody. The bandmaster was evidently the Holy Spirit. He can render music without rehearsals on a company of yielded instruments. Glory!
(Maria Woodworth-Etter)[21]

Heaven is full of music! During the face-to-face encounter I described earlier, I was intensely aware of the exquisitely beautiful songs that the angels were singing.

Because music touches a different hemisphere of the brain, it impacts us in ways that words alone can not. It has been central in almost every revival and helps us to identify with the people and places the Lord is laying on our heart.[22]

'The devil flees before the sound of music faster than from anything except the Word of God,' Martin Luther declared – in which case, let us seek out ways of putting music and the Word together to take us deeper in the flow of the Lord's leading.

One of the most lovely things the Lord is doing in our time is to raise up modern day psalmists. As they express the beauty of the Lord in songs of adoration, and His heart through music that releases His power, we may suddenly find that we are, as it were, able to overhear the plans and conversations that are being carried on in the council of the Lord.

We experienced a striking example of this when one of our lead singers was given a beautiful prophetic song, 'To those who seek His face, I will reveal My heart.' Moments later we were crying out to the Lord on behalf of children who had been abused. The Lord then gave the worship group what I can only describe as a 'wall of sound,' into which were woven the screams and cries of the children. This led us as perhaps nothing else could ever have done into sharing more fully in how the Lord feels about this most grievous of sins.

The Lord then gave another anointed singer a powerful lament in an Arabic-sounding tongue. It was a perfect imitation of the music that is commonly intoned from minaret towers. Coming from a Christian, it was nothing less than the call of the Lord to the women of Islam to know Him as He really is.

The Lord has a wonderful sense of occasion. Dates and anniversaries are important to Him as well as to us. I was privileged to minister at a special service in Dresden on the 50th anniversary of the bombing of the city. At the hour when the first wave of bombers dropped their lethal load, killing up to 100,000 people, shofars (rams-horns) sounded their extraordinary wail. We lifted up our hearts and voices and prayed for forgiveness to flow between Britain, America and Germany – and for angels to come where bombs had once fallen. It was one of God's special reconciliation moments.

I remember a meeting in Wales, where we physically divided the conference into those who were English, and those who were authentically Welsh. When the English repented of all the pain that we have inflicted on the Welsh over the centuries, the Welsh people present responded by praying that the resentment they feel as a nation as a result of this suffering be taken from them. We then moved across the divide to embrace each other. It was a precious and powerful symbol of a much-needed reconciliation. May the tide of prayer that is rising rapidly for Wales overcome the power and anger that fuels so much of Welsh nationalism through the love and power of Christ. God is hearing these prayers!

Something similar happened during a day of prayer at a YWAM base for Scotland. The Lord gave us a powerful flow of intercession for the nation, in which we were able to express our repentance for the many hurts that we, the English, have inflicted through the centuries. We felt the Lord's grief at all the creativity the country had been robbed of, and thrilled to the exquisite music the Spirit inspired: music that captured the very essence of all the Lord intends Scotland to be.

This is by no means a new phenomenon. Back in 657, a tone deaf farm laborer in the north of England used to dread the long winter evenings that his fellow workers passed singing and creating ballads. Whenever he could see his turn approaching he would disappear into one of the stables.

One night, an angel met him in his stable and told him to sing. Caedmon protested that he really was no good at it, but the angel overrode his objections and ordered him to sing. Caedmon opened his mouth and began to sing about creation.[23] The words and music were so powerful that, when the moment Abbess Hilda heard them, she promptly took him into her monastery at Whitby, in order to develop the gift the Lord had given him. Caedmon became known throughout Northumbria, for his stirring songs, by means of which he taught people the ways of God.

How different all this is from any idea of a few packaged songs 'before the preacher gets on with the real work.' May the Lord raise up more and more singers and musicians to make full use of this precious means of communicating the heart of God with us.

Once, when I was speaking on the theme of spiritual warfare, and finding the going tough, my two fellow leaders slipped out to telephone home for prayer support of 'Wives Net.' Within seconds the atmosphere began to lift.

God can do extraordinary things through music. In the worship at the end of that meeting, several people commented on how beautiful the flute playing was. One specified that it was a wooden flute. Nothing unusual about that – except that there was no flautist present! Nearly a hundred miles away, however, one of the leader's wives had begun to intercede – and was playing her wooden flute for us.

The Lord wants us to move far beyond the traditional pattern of the worship group, the intercessor and the teacher, all remaining as separate ministries in their own self-contained slots. The Church is not a roll-on roll-off ferry that needs such watertight compartments. It is so much more exciting if we are able to weave praise, worship, prayer and teaching together as a 'seamless garment,' the one fueling and inspiring the other.

More than fifty years ago, C.S. Lewis declared that if Europe is to be touched again by God, then it will be through a revival of music and the performing arts. We read in books such as Samuel, Chronicles and the Psalms of musicians doing things that we are only now beginning to see them doing again. David played the harp to ward off a demonic spirit that was plaguing the reigning king; Elisha sent for a lutist in a desperate military crisis, and then received a prophetic word that saved the combined armies of Israel and Judah.

These examples are more than just special one-offs that God did in the distant past: they have a direct relevance to what He wants to do in our own situation today. May the Lord anoint His people to be infinitely creative in such ways.

For Reflection and Prayer

Lord, as we weave music, worship and intercession,
may Your Presence draw near
May Your Still Small Voice speak to Your people.
and the glory of Jesus be known
through all who sing and make music for You.
Release power and wisdom
through the preachers, writers,
artists and producers
whom You are raising up.

Direct their attention to themes
that reflect Your heart.
Let the touch of Heaven be
on all that is spoken,
written or created in Your name.
In Jesus' name, Amen.

Further on and Further in

And there lay a little old woman . . . She was at death's door, but when she opened her eyes and saw the bright, hairy head of the lion staring into her face, she did not scream or faint. She said, 'Oh Aslan! . . . I've been waiting for this all my life. Have you come to take me away?' 'Yes, Dearest,' said Aslan. 'But not the long journey yet.'[24]

I love Aslan's words in the concluding Chronicle of Narnia: 'Further on and further in!'[25] However much we may have experienced already, the Lord has more in store for us.

As we advance along the path the Lord has laid out for us, we find that He has gone ahead, to anoint us for fresh endeavors, and to reward us for assignments faithfully accomplished.

It is no sign of second best, however, if we are only able to discern the Lord's leading when we look back on something in retrospect.

Neither should we consider ourselves 'second rate' if we do not hear the Lord in the ways I have set out in this book. With the Lord it is never a matter of 'either or' but rather of 'both and.'

In many contexts, to show love and kindness to others is far more important than 'hearing' a word from the Lord for them – just as in other situations nothing but a word from the Lord will suffice to bring about a breakthrough.

Neither can we perpetuate or preserve the Still Small Voice, any more than Peter could prolong the experience on the Mount of Transfiguration, or Mary could keep hold of the Lord Jesus in the garden after the Resurrection.[26] What we can and must do is to abide in Him.

Pressures and distractions are sure to abound, but we must continue to follow His leading, rather than consulting our personal likes or dislikes – or our bank balance for that matter. We were never meant to rely on our own unaided efforts and resources.

'*Do not throw away your confidence,*' the Scriptures urges us; '*it will be rewarded.*'[27] He will not fail to find surprising ways to accomplish all that He has promised.

As he neared his homecoming, the Lord spoke to David Watson. 'All your writing and all your preaching are as nothing compared with your relationship with Me.'[28]

This is a fitting emphasis on which to draw this book to a close. On a Parisian Metro station, back in the mid 1970's, I had just said goodbye to a fellowship that had meant a great deal to me. I was feeling an almost overwhelming feeling of loss and was singing under my breath, 'O Jesus I have promised, to serve Thee to the end.'

Suddenly, I was engulfed in a profound sense of the Lord's presence. For a prolonged moment the presence of Heaven drew close, and it was as though I heard an astonishing echo: 'And I have promised to serve you to the end.'

How great He is, that He stoops down to serve His children. Therefore we can rest in the love that has supported us all the days of our life, and embark with confidence on all that He has called us to be and to do.

May you always have the courage to step out with what you believe God is saying to you. Despite the risks and the potential embarrassment, He honors those who honor Him!

For Reflection and Prayer

High King of Heaven,
You release that which is deadlocked.
and raise the dead to life.
May there never be a day when we fail to seek Your face
or do something to advance Your Kingdom,
as we commit ourselves to the adventure
of following Your Still Small Voice.

Draw the sting of every hurt we have sustained,
every disappointment that weighs us down,
every situation that remains unresolved,
and turn them round for Your glory.
Let no residue of bitterness cloud our minds
as we push in Your name through every obstacle
until what You have promised comes to pass.

Immerse us now in the depths of Your love.
Quiet our minds from care and worry,
ward off danger and keep us from evil.
As we soak in the life that is really life,
may Your angels guard and guide
each day that we live for You,
and cleanse the stream of our thoughts.

Lord of Glory,
Put fears and fancies to flight.
Settle our spirits in the Peace of all Peace,
in the full awareness of the host of Heaven.
In the name of the Father, who calls and sustains us,
The Prince of Peace, who gives life to our souls, and
The Spirit of Power, who directs our days.

References

[1] As the Spirit prompts, it can also be really powerful to pray with pre-Christians. It allows them to experience the presence of the Lord and the practice of prayer.

[2] Derek Prince *Shaping History through Prayer and Fasting* (Spire Books)

[3] I wrote *Praying Together* (Sovereign World) to help churches and prayer groups understand some of the practicalities and the dynamics that are involved when people come to pray together. We need to give considerable thought to this matter of rounding up and harnessing prayer.

[4] Rigobertu Menchu tells how hurt the people of Guatemala feel when visitors admire the costumes that they wear, but treat the people wearing them as if they did not exist.

[5] John 1:50 and 5:20

[6] Acts 16:18, cf 13:8-12; 3:6, 20:9-11, 28:8-10

[7] C S Lewis, *The Magician's Nephew*, (Harper Collins) p.169

[8] Here are some 'starter' passages which hint at how passionately God feels about certain things that are wrong: 1 Samuel 15:11;Exodus 32; Revelation chapters 2-3.

[9] Matthew 14:14, 15:32, 20:34; Mark 1:41, 6:34, 8:2; Luke 7:13-15.

[10] Romans 8:26

[11] See Ecclesiastes 7:2-4

[12] John 11:33

[13] Hebrews 13:3

[14] Ezekiel 9:3-6; cf 2 Peter 2:7-8

[15] Jeremiah 9:1

[16] James O. Fraser, *Mountain Rain* (Paternoster Publishing)

[17] James Rutz, *Megashift* (Empowerment Press, Colorado Springs) p. 62

[18] Rutz lists for starters: alcoholism, multiple divorces, poverty, domestic abuse, emotional deadness, and criminal acts that trickle down to the third and fourth generation. He also encourages us to check out Exodus 34:9, Leviticus 26:40-42, Ezra 9:1-15; Nehemiah 1:4-7 and 9:1-2, Psalm 106:6, Jeremiah 3:25 and 32:18; Ezekiel 4:4-7; Daniel 9:3-11 cf Colossians 1:24; Romans 9:1-3, 10:1; Ezekiel 4:4-17 – but see also Ezekiel 18:20 and Jeremiah 31:29-30 for a balance. See also John Dawson, *Healing America's Wounds* (Regal Books).

[19] Norman Grubb *Rees Howells, Intercessor* (Lutterworth).

[20] Hebrews 5:7

[21] Maria Woodworth-Etter *Signs and Wonders* (Whitaker House) p. 256

[22] No wonder that so many are seeking to develop 'music therapy' as a way of curing everything from epilepsy to autism. But even music is not an end in itself so much as a way into God's presence. To avoid getting stuck in any tradition (even a good one) it can be good to find ways to worship from time to time without using music – for instance through pictures, photographs and the creative use of fabrics.

[23] Despite the vicissitudes of the British climate, and the endless Viking raids that destroyed so much Christian material, we still possess the openings lines of this song that the Lord entrusted to Caedmon. It has long been treasured as the earliest surviving poem in the Old English dialect.

[24] C.S.Lewis, *Prince Caspian* (Harper Collins). p. 219

[25] C.S. Lewis, *The Last Battle* (Harper Collins).

[26] John 20:17

[27] Hebrews 10:35

[28] David Watson *Fear No Evil* (Hodder & Stoughton).

Some books you may find helpful

Cooke, Graham *Crafted Prayer: The Joy of Always Getting Your Prayers Answered* (Chosen Books)

Deare, Jack *Surprised by the Voice of God* (Kingsway)

Foster, Richard *Freedom of Simplicity* (Hodder and Stoughton) *Prayer: Finding the Heart's True Home* (Harper Collins)

Fraser, James *Mountain Rain* (Paternoster Publishing)

Grubb, Norman *Rees Howells, Intercessor* (Lutterworth)

Hurnard, Hannah *The Hearing Heart* (Mass Market Paperbacks) (Out of print but can be tracked down on the Internet).

Huggett, Joyce *Listening to God* (Hodder)

MacDonald, Gordon *Restoring Your Spiritual Passion* (Highland)

Marshall, Tom *Understanding Leadership,* (Sovereign World)

Mumford, Bob *Take Another Look at Guidance* (Life-changers); *The Purpose of Temptation* (Bridge Publishers Inc.)

Nouwen, Henri *The Genesee Diary* (Darton Longman & Todd Ltd.)

Payne, Leanne – Various books: all highly recommended

Prince, Derek *Shaping History through Prayer and Fasting* (Spire Books)

Renner, Rick *Sparkling Gems from the Greek* (Teach All Nations) Outstanding

Rutz, James *Megashift* (Empowerment Press, Colorado)

Sandford, John and Paula *The Elijah Task* (Victory House Publishers); *Elijah Among us* (Chosen Books)

Watson, David *Fear no Evil* (Hodder)

Weston, Robert *Praying Together* (Sovereign World), *Ravens and the Prophet* (New Wine), *Intimacy and Eternity* (New Wine) Available via www.ruachministries.org (Articles and Publications).

Wilkinson, Bruce *The Prayer of Jabez* (Multnomah).

The Pilgrim's Guides

Still Small Voice is the first in a planned series of publications. *Led by the Spirit* will explore the lives and ministries of many of the biblical prophets, and then go on to provide practical insights into aspects of the prophetic ministry. A message for our times, it will help us to make sense of what the Lord is saying to us today.

Other planned titles in The Pilgrim's Guide Series include:

Veil of Tears ~ Coping with Grief, written for those who are in mourning themselves, as well as for those who are coming alongside those who are grieving.

The Wilderness ~ Exile or Epicenter? will explore different types of spiritual wildernesses, and discover how the Lord would have us welcome those that come from Him, resist those that do not, and learn from those that are the consequence of our own foolishness!

Join us for the journey – and may God greatly bless you on it!

Write to Robert Weston

c/o Mowbray Lodge, Marshbrook,

Church Stretton, Shropshire, SY6 6QE, England

rrweston@rrweston.f9.co.uk

www.ruachministries.org

Robert Weston has a special gift from God to put into words what our heart knows, but has never focused on, or known how to express. These insights from God's heart cause us to say with excitement, "Yes! This is something I want to remember and make a part of my life forever!"

(Rosalie Willis, www.acompanyofwomen.org)